the ski house
cookbook

the ski house cookbook

warm winter dishes for cold weather fun

TINA ANDERSON and SARAH PINNEO

CLARKSON POTTER/PUBLISHERS
New York

Published in the United States by Clarkson Potter/Publishers,
an imprint of the Crown Publishing Group,
a division of Random House, Inc., New York.
www.crownpublishing.com
www.clarksonpotter.com

Clarkson N. Potter is a trademark and Potter and colophon
are registered trademarks of Random House, Inc.

Library of Congress Cataloging-in-Publication Data
Anderson, Tina.
    The ski house cookbook: warm winter dishes for cold weather
fun / Tina Anderson and Sarah Pinneo—1st ed.
    Includes index.
    1. Cookery.   I. Pinneo, Sarah.   II. Title.
TX714.P555   2007
641.5—dc22   2006037002

ISBN 978-0-307-33998-0

Printed in Singapore

Design by Maggie Hinders
Prop stylist: Christina Lane
Food stylist: Margarette Adams

10   9   8   7   6   5   4   3   2   1

First Edition

contents

acknowledgments

THANK YOU to our family, friends, and tasters for their unwavering support of our cooking endeavors. Thank you Mike, Jack, and Wyatt for eating braised pork shoulder four nights in a row. Special thanks to David Prince, Christina Lane, and Margarette Adams for helping us bring our recipes to life. Finally, thank you to our agent, Carla Glasser, for seeing the potential in us and in our idea, and to our editor, Rica Allannic, for taking a chance. And to all the skiers out there: Safety first!

introduction

WE GREW UP IN SNOW—lots of it—in Western Michigan. The average low temperature in January is 16 degrees, and "lake effect"—gray clouds rolling off Lake Michigan and dumping their chilly contents onto the streets of our youth—is more than a feature of the weather: It is a way of life. The landscape is, unfortunately, completely flat. Sometimes it seems the six months of winter are spent either waiting for the car to heat up or shoveling the walk.

Our love of winter was born when we found skiing. We discovered that the view from a mountaintop and a bit of the right gear could keep us outside for hours without feeling too cold. We learned that pointing our tips down the hill felt like flying, and that red cheeks and hat head were charming in the right venue.

We love to ski, and we also love to cook. And when we ski, we cook up a storm. What's the link? First, we're starved. There is something about breathing cold air all day and tearing around at great speed that makes for a healthy appetite. (Exercise specialists will tell you that skiing isn't terribly aerobic, since gravity does a lot of the work for you, but we know better.)

Another reason we cook is that wintertime demands that we celebrate our good fortune to spend the day outside with a restorative feast. While we don't think anyone really needs a grand excuse to sup on chili or wintry braised meats, 'tis the season.

Finally, there are practical matters. Finding a great meal in a ski town can be downright challenging. Unless you're someplace terribly cosmopolitan like Aspen, Colorado, or Park City, Utah, you may be skiing the terrain of champions but confined to less than regal restaurant choices. To put it nicely, many rural ski towns aren't known for their haute cuisine. And if you are lucky enough to find yourself in a really swish locale, make sure you've got reservations and a fat wallet. When everyone in town is enjoying the same schedule, those fancy restaurants are packed—and with demand outstripping supply, they can and do charge whatever they please.

Some of us have kids. Marching them all to a crowded eatery, waiting for a table, ordering carefully to accommodate little tastes, and sitting through dinner is sometimes more than we can bear. There's always pizza . . . but in many places ordering a pizza is the culinary equivalent of being carried down the mountain on the ski patrol sled: If you can avoid it, you should.

For all these reasons, we deemed it necessary to bring you *The Ski House Cookbook*, with our version of the best ways to enjoy the culinary accompaniments to the downhill life. Having done a lot of ski house cooking, we have a few tricks to share. We like to eat as if we've spent the day in the kitchen without actually having done so. This can mean the slow cooker works hard all day so you don't have to, as in the case of our Mogul Beef Chili. Or it can mean preparing calzones ahead of time, freezing them, and popping them in the oven when we get home.

Luckily, many main-course foods taste best when they are cooked either very quickly, like steaks, or very slowly, like braised pork shoulder. We've taken every possible advantage of this fact, not only for main courses but also for breakfast, lunch, snacks, side dishes, and desserts. Given the limited resources you might find in an underequipped ski house kitchen, no electric mixers, mandolines, or multiple pans are called for here.

Above all, ski house cooking should be easy. While we may love to *dine* upon duck confit with black truffle sauce, we don't consider fussy preparations requiring hard-to-find ingredients reasonable after a full day outdoors.

We rely on pantry items for ease of storage and because shopping opportunities are limited in many out-of-the-way towns. We won't send you to the local minimart for fenugreek. We also don't like to rely on out-of-season produce; while we love basil, for example, we prefer in this book to take advantage of ingredients associated with the colder months of the year. We use herbs and spices that dry well, but also the root vegetables and aged cheeses that really taste like wintertime.

Finally, ski house cooking should also be scalable; some of these recipes are a good choice for two, and some work for ten. This food is meant to be savored with family and friends, whether close family or a complete racing team.

The Ratings

We rate our recipes with a nod to ski trail ratings: green circles for the easiest, blue squares for those that are moderately difficult, and black diamonds for dishes that require a little more effort. We don't have any *double* black diamond recipes; we'd rather save that effort for the slopes.

The ratings system is meant to consider many factors; not only does it reflect the difficulty of assembling the dish but also the prep time involved, the number and availability of ingredients, and the cost. Thus, our recipe for peanut butter cookies, which calls for five pantry ingredients, is a beginner's trail, compared to coconut macaroons dipped in chocolate, which have more ingredients and more steps. We consider those an intermediate slope. Because we like to eat well without living in the kitchen, you may notice that we don't offer many recipes labeled "for experts only." Unlike some of our favorite Vermont ski resorts, we don't believe in grade inflation. We think you'll be satisfied with yourself and your food even if we call the dish what it is—a groomer.

Whether you've spent your day skiing, riding, or shoveling, we feel sure you will find what you're looking for here. We'll see you down at the lift.

breakfast

OUR MOTHERS ALWAYS TOLD US that breakfast was the most important meal of the day. When the day will include bombing down a 30-degree slope through the trees, Mom might have been right. It is a long way to the bottom. If you're not careful, you'll end up standing in front of one of those slope-side waffle sheds—the ones that pump the irresistible smell of charred sugar into the air and then part you from the contents of your wallet for a hot waffle and a bottle of water.

These recipes prove that you can enjoy a speedy breakfast and still get in a full day of skiing. We like to hit the trails early—before the crowds arrive and while the snow is still pristine. To that end, the majority of our breakfast recipes are all about efficiency. It came as a revelation to us that we could assemble a savory egg dish or French toast the night before and then serve it hot out of the oven without hassle when we woke up. Now we'd hardly consider going back to the old-fashioned way of whisking and dipping and standing by the griddle all morning.

If you want to take your breakfast with you on the way to the mountain, baked goods are the obvious choice. Muffins, either hearty Apple–Raisin Bran Muffins or cakey Super Sour-Cream Muffins, tuck easily into a sack or pocket. Those with a sweet tooth might choose Cinnamon Streusel Coffee Cake or Quick Pains au Chocolat instead.

On the other hand, if the weather isn't cooperating or you were up late the night before, it might be a good day to linger over breakfast. Choose decadent Eggs Benedict with Chipotle Hollandaise, Huevos Rancheros, or Blueberry Buttermilk Pancakes. A large pot of coffee and a half-day ticket might be in your future.

● 'twas the night before french toast

WHILE WE LOVE FRENCH TOAST, we don't love the inevitable eating in shifts that results from cooking batches in one skillet. Much like waiting in the wind at the peak for friends on the next chairlift, it isn't as social as we'd like. We solve the problem by baking rather than frying. Prepare this dish the night before and pop it in the oven while you're suiting up; then you can enjoy a delicious breakfast and still make first tracks. (Purists may point out that the recipe is essentially for a breakfast bread pudding. Whatever you call it, this dish is both easy and wonderful.)

1. The night before you wish to serve the dish, butter a heavy roasting pan, 9 x 13 inches or larger. If you have large loaves of bread, cut them into slices $3/4$ inch thick and arrange the slices in the pan so they overlap slightly. If you have commercially sliced bread that is thinner than $3/4$ inch, cut the slices on the diagonal and generously overlap them in the pan. If you have a baguette, cut the slices 1 inch thick and arrange them in one tight layer in the pan.

2. In a large bowl, combine the eggs, milk, nutmeg, vanilla, and $1/2$ cup of the sugar. Whisk until well combined. Pour the mixture evenly over the bread slices. Cover the pan with plastic wrap or foil and refrigerate overnight or for at least 3 hours.

3. Center a rack in the oven and preheat to 400°F. Mix the remaining $1/4$ cup sugar with the cinnamon. Uncover the pan and sprinkle the sugar mixture on top. Follow with the butter, and then the pecans and blueberries.

4. Bake for 30 to 40 minutes, depending on the size of the pan, until the bread is golden brown and the berry juices are bubbling. The French toast may puff up in the oven and then fall back to its original height while it cools. Serve slices warm, with or without syrup.

SERVES 6 TO 8

1 (1-pound) loaf Italian bread, brioche, large dense baguette, or other dense white bread

5 large eggs

$2^1/2$ cups whole milk

$1/2$ teaspoon ground nutmeg

1 teaspoon vanilla extract

$3/4$ cup (packed) light brown sugar

$1/4$ teaspoon ground cinnamon

3 tablespoons unsalted butter, melted, plus more for the pan

1 cup pecans (about 3 ounces), coarsely chopped

$1^1/2$ cups frozen blueberries or mixed berries

Maple syrup (optional)

b is for better

THE SYRUP SHELVES in the grocery store can be confusing to contemplate. Here is some basic advice: When you see bottles, including most of the nationally known brands, marked "breakfast syrup," walk away. Don't even make eye contact.

In our opinion, the only syrup worth consuming is pure maple syrup. It is made simply, with just one ingredient. Early in the spring, maple trees are tapped, and the watery sap runs into buckets or into a line system for collection. This sap is boiled down to about one-fortieth of its original volume to make pure maple syrup.

The only complicated task is choosing among the thousands of brands and bottles. Most syrup is made by tiny producers literally in the front yards of rural homes in Vermont and other New England states. The U.S. Department of Agriculture (USDA) has four grades for maple syrup, which are supposed to help the consumer figure out what is in the bottle. The grades are sorted by color, which is a good indication of how strongly flavored the syrups are.

* GRADE A LIGHT, also called Fancy Grade, is often produced at the beginning of the sugaring season. It has the mildest flavor and the highest price tag. We feel that Grade A Light syrup is for tourists and wimps. Why pay extra to get less maple flavor?

* GRADE A MEDIUM AMBER is the next darkest. Much of the syrup sold fits into this category. It has a richer maple flavor than the light variety.

* GRADE A DARK AMBER is even darker and more flavorful.

* GRADE B is the darkest of all, with the most maple flavor and a nutty, caramel aspect. Some folks call Grade B cooking syrup and use it only to flavor foods, not as a table syrup. We think this is a mistake. More flavor is better.

No matter which you choose, be assured that there are no purity differences among the grades—just differences in color and flavor. Although we think that the inexpensive Grade B is the best way to go, the decision is really a matter of taste. (We don't really like light beers either, but that's another story.)

Store opened syrup in the refrigerator. It will keep more than three months before mold begins to form and the syrup must be thrown away.

● blueberry buttermilk pancakes

INNOVATION IS NOT ALWAYS IMPROVEMENT. For example, battery-powered boot warmers are a great idea on paper, but they don't work well in practice. This is why we swear by the classic flavor of tender buttermilk pancakes. Dressed up with blueberries, they are perfect.

---

1. In a large bowl, whisk together the flour, sugar, baking powder, baking soda, and salt. In a medium bowl, whisk together the eggs, buttermilk, and melted butter. Pour the wet ingredients into the dry ingredients and stir just until combined.

2. Heat a large nonstick skillet or griddle over medium heat. Brush lightly with butter. When the skillet is hot, pour in $1/4$ cup batter for each pancake, leaving room for the pancakes to spread. Sprinkle the tops with blueberries. Cook until small bubbles appear on the surface and the bottoms are golden, 2 to 3 minutes. Flip the pancakes and cook until golden, another 1 to 2 minutes. Repeat with the remaining batter, adding butter to the pan as needed. Serve immediately with maple syrup.

MAKES 10 (4-INCH) PANCAKES

$1^1/_2$ cups all-purpose flour

2 tablespoons sugar

2 teaspoons baking powder

$^1/_2$ teaspoon baking soda

$^1/_4$ teaspoon salt

2 large eggs

$1^3/_4$ cups buttermilk

3 tablespoons unsalted butter, melted, plus more for cooking

1 cup fresh or frozen blueberries

Maple syrup

■ oatmeal pancakes with sautéed cinnamon apples

PACKED WITH WHOLE GRAINS, these pancakes will keep you going all morning long. Even better, they taste great and have a nutty flavor that goes nicely with warm apple slices.

1. In a large bowl, whisk together the oats, flour, wheat germ, sugar, baking powder, cinnamon, and salt. Whisk in the egg and milk until just combined.

2. Heat a large nonstick skillet or griddle over medium heat. Brush lightly with butter. When the skillet is hot, pour in 1/4 cup batter for each pancake, leaving room for the pancakes to spread. Cook until small bubbles appear on the surface and the bottoms are golden, about 2 minutes. Flip the pancakes and cook until golden, about 1 minute. Repeat with the remaining batter, adding butter to the pan as needed. Serve immediately, topped with the apples.

MAKES 10 (4-INCH) PANCAKES

1/2 cup old-fashioned rolled oats

1/2 cup whole wheat flour

2 tablespoons wheat germ

2 tablespoons light brown sugar

2 teaspoons baking powder

1/4 teaspoon ground cinnamon

1/4 teaspoon salt

1 large egg, lightly beaten

1 cup whole milk

Unsalted butter

Sautéed Cinnamon Apples (recipe follows)

sautéed cinnamon apples

Melt the butter in a medium skillet over medium heat. Add the sugar and stir with a wooden spoon to dissolve. Add the apples, walnuts, and cinnamon and cook for 6 minutes, or until the apples are soft. Serve warm over pancakes or oatmeal.

MAKES ABOUT 2 CUPS

2 tablespoons unsalted butter

2 tablespoons brown sugar

2 medium apples, peeled, cored, and sliced

1/4 cup chopped walnuts

1/4 teaspoon ground cinnamon

● maple-glazed bacon

WE'RE FANS OF BACON, but not of scrubbing a grease-spattered cooktop before skiing. So we prepare it in the oven, where the mess is at least contained, if not eliminated. The sweet maple glaze used here turns an ordinary breakfast item into a truly divine day-starter.

---

1. Preheat the oven to 375°F.

2. Arrange the bacon slices in one layer on a rimmed baking sheet or in a roasting pan. Brush the syrup onto the bacon slices. (If you're using brown sugar, mix it with 2 teaspoons of water in a teacup and then brush it on.)

3. Bake for 6 to 7 minutes. Using tongs or a fork, flip each strip of bacon and cook for an additional 3 to 5 minutes or until crisp.

4. Remove the bacon to drain on paper towels for a minute or two before serving.

SERVES 4 TO 6

12 ounces thick-cut bacon (about 12 slices)

1 tablespoon maple syrup or 1 tablespoon brown sugar

NOTE The cooking time for bacon is highly dependent on the thickness of the slices. If you are using slices that are less than 1 ounce each, check the bacon frequently to avoid burning.

■ huevos rancheros

IN MOST WESTERN SKI TOWNS, you can't swing a ski pole without hitting a plateful of this savory, hearty breakfast. Luckily, it is easy to whip up at home. We'll help you avoid the crowds at the diner, if not at the ski lift.

─────────────────────────

1. Place the tomatoes and their juice, the onion, garlic, and chipotle in a blender and puree until smooth. Transfer the mixture to a medium saucepan and place over medium heat. Bring to a simmer. Add ¼ teaspoon salt and cook for 5 minutes. Remove from the heat and keep warm until ready to serve.

2. Meanwhile, in a large nonstick skillet, heat the oil over medium-high heat. Fry the tortillas one at a time, 20 seconds per side. Drain them on paper towels.

3. Reduce the heat to medium-low, add the butter, and let melt. Carefully break 4 of the eggs into the skillet. Cover and cook until set, about 2 minutes. Sprinkle with salt and pepper. Transfer to a plate and keep warm. Repeat with the remaining eggs.

4. Place the tortillas on plates and spread sauce on them. Sprinkle with cheese and top each tortilla with 2 fried eggs. Ladle additional sauce around the tortillas. Garnish with chopped cilantro, if desired, and serve immediately.

SERVES 4

1 (14-ounce) can diced tomatoes

1 small onion, chopped

2 garlic cloves

1 canned chipotle pepper in adobo sauce

Salt

1 tablespoon vegetable oil

4 (6-inch) corn tortillas

1 tablespoon unsalted butter

8 large eggs

Freshly ground black pepper

1 cup (4 ounces) shredded Monterey Jack

¼ cup chopped fresh cilantro (optional)

◆ eggs benedict with chipotle hollandaise

CLASSIC EGGS BENEDICT HAVE THEIR PLACE, but making the hollandaise sauce can be intimidating. The blender method of preparation reduces the fear factor. These eggs Benedict have a Mexican twist, fired up with chipotle peppers and served over corn bread for a Southwestern taste.

---

1. To poach the eggs: In a large saucepan, bring 2 inches of water and the vinegar to a boil. Reduce the heat so that the water simmers gently. Break 1 egg into a small bowl. Carefully tip the bowl, allowing the egg to slide gently into the water. Repeat with the remaining eggs. Cook for 3 to 4 minutes, until the whites are firm and the yolks are just set but still runny in the middle. Carefully remove the eggs with a slotted spoon and transfer to paper towels to drain.

2. To make the sauce: Combine the yolks, lemon juice, and hot water in a blender. Blend for 1 minute. With the blender running, slowly and carefully pour the hot butter through the open hole of the blender lid. Blend for 1 minute. Add the chipotle pepper and a pinch of salt and pepper and blend for 30 more seconds or until smooth. Keep warm until ready to serve.

3. In a nonstick skillet, heat the bacon until warmed through.

4. Slice the squares of corn bread in half horizontally to create 4 equal squares. Place the squares on plates and top each with 1 slice of bacon and 1 poached egg. Pour the warm sauce over the top and serve immediately.

NOTE You can easily adapt the recipe to your taste by including more peppers than called for or not using them at all. Serve on toasted English muffin halves if you don't have corn bread on hand.

SERVES 4

2 teaspoons vinegar

4 large eggs

3 large egg yolks

1 tablespoon fresh lemon juice

1 tablespoon hot water

10 tablespoons unsalted butter, melted and hot

1 canned chipotle pepper in adobo sauce

Salt and freshly ground black pepper

4 slices Canadian bacon

2 (4-inch) squares Buttermilk Corn Bread (page 147) or store-bought corn bread

● ham and cheddar breakfast strata

YOU MAY WANT TO SERVE EGGS TO A CROWD, but perhaps you aren't sure you can expertly fold a ten-egg omelet while everyone watches—the culinary equivalent of tackling those mogul runs right under the lift. We don't blame you. This dish is the perfect solution: You mix it up the night before and then bake it in the morning. You'll look like an expert, plunking down a bubbling brunch dish with less effort than it takes to fill the juice glasses.

1. The night before you wish to serve the strata, combine the eggs, milk, mustard, and salt in a medium bowl. Whisk until thoroughly blended.

2. In another medium bowl, mix the ham, bell pepper, scallions, onion, and 1 cup of the cheese.

3. Butter a 9 x 13-inch baking dish. Place half of the bread on the bottom of the dish in one layer. Scatter half of the ham mixture over the bread. Repeat, using the remaining bread and ham mixture.

4. Pour the egg mixture evenly over the top. Cover and refrigerate overnight or for at least 1 hour.

5. Preheat the oven to 375°F.

6. Uncover the strata and bake for 45 to 50 minutes, or until the center is just set. Sprinkle the remaining cheese on top and bake for an additional 10 minutes, or until bubbling and beginning to brown.

7. Cut into squares and serve hot or at room temperature.

SERVES 6 TO 8

10 large eggs

$1^3/_4$ cups whole milk

1 tablespoon plus 1 teaspoon Dijon mustard

$1/_2$ teaspoon salt

2 cups cubed ham steak (about 10 ounces)

1 red bell pepper, cored, seeded, and diced

8 scallions, white and light green parts, thinly sliced

1 small onion, diced

$1^1/_2$ cups shredded sharp Cheddar (about 6 ounces)

Unsalted butter

6 cups cubed sourdough sandwich bread (about $1/_2$ loaf)

● super sour-cream muffins

MUFFINS BAKE UP QUICKLY, are easily portable, and have a built-in portion-control mechanism ... unless you bring along the whole batch. Muffin batters are similar from recipe to recipe, the main difference being the liquid ingredient. We like sour cream for the flavor it imparts and the cakelike texture it gives the muffins.

---

1. Preheat the oven to 375°F. Butter a standard 12-cup muffin tin and set aside.

2. In a large bowl, stir together the flour, baking powder, baking soda, and salt.

3. In a medium bowl, whisk together the egg, sugar, 8 tablespoons butter, and the vanilla. Whisk in the sour cream.

4. Make a well in the center of the dry ingredients. Pour the wet ingredients into the dry ingredients and stir just to combine. Do not over-mix. Divide the batter evenly in the muffin tin and sprinkle the tops with sugar.

5. Bake until golden, about 20 minutes. (A toothpick inserted into the center of a muffin should come out clean.) Cool the muffins in the pan on a rack for about 10 minutes. Remove the muffins from the pan to the rack to continue cooling. Serve warm or at room temperature.

❋ BLUEBERRY MUFFINS

Add 1 teaspoon grated lemon zest to the wet ingredients in step 3. Gently fold in 1 cup fresh or frozen blueberries after mixing the batter in step 4.

❋ CRANBERRY-ORANGE MUFFINS

Add 2 teaspoons grated orange zest to the wet ingredients in step 3. Gently fold in 1 cup chopped fresh cranberries (or 3/4 cup dried) after mixing the batter in step 4.

MAKES 12 MUFFINS

2 cups all-purpose flour

1 tablespoon baking powder

1/2 teaspoon baking soda

1/2 teaspoon salt

1 large egg

3/4 cup sugar, plus more for garnish

8 tablespoons unsalted butter (1 stick), melted, plus more for the pan

1/2 teaspoon vanilla extract

1 cup sour cream

■ apple–raisin bran muffins

THIS IS THE HEALTHIEST MUFFIN RECIPE we actually love. It is very low in sugar and features two whole grains. These muffins are terrific just out of the oven, with a dense, hearty character. They are not cupcakes disguised as breakfast! Chopping the apple adds to the preparation time, but the results are worth it.

1. Preheat the oven to 400°F. Butter a standard 12-cup muffin tin and set aside.

2. Combine the cereal and milk in a medium bowl and set aside to soften for 5 minutes.

3. In a large bowl, whisk the egg. Add the sugar and the 8 table-spoons melted butter. Whisk to combine. Stir in the softened cereal and the apples.

4. In a medium bowl, stir together the all-purpose flour, whole wheat flour, baking powder, cinnamon, ginger, and salt. Add this mixture to the wet ingredients and stir until just moistened. The batter will be thick and lumpy.

5. Spoon the batter evenly into the muffin tin. The 12 cups will be quite full.

6. Bake for 20 to 25 minutes, or until the tops of the muffins begin to brown. Remove the pan to a cooling rack for 5 minutes. When the muffins are cool enough to handle, tip them onto a plate. Serve warm.

MAKES 12 MUFFINS

2 cups Raisin Bran or Bran Flakes cereal

1 cup whole milk

1 large egg

$1/3$ cup (firmly packed) dark brown sugar

8 tablespoons (1 stick) unsalted butter, melted and cooled, plus more for the pan

$1^1/2$ cups peeled and finely diced apples (from 1 to 2 tart apples)

$3/4$ cup all-purpose flour

$1/2$ cup whole wheat flour or all-purpose

1 tablespoon baking powder

$1/2$ teaspoon ground cinnamon

$1/2$ teaspoon ground ginger

$1/4$ teaspoon salt

● quick pains au chocolat

THESE LITTLE GEMS address the age-old problem of how to get more chocolate into your morning. Serve them with steaming cups of café au lait before you head out into the cold.

1. Preheat the oven to 375°F.

2. Brush one edge of a puff pastry square with the egg wash. Place 1 tablespoon chocolate on the opposite edge of the pastry square and roll the dough tightly toward the egg wash side. Press the edge with the egg wash into the dough to seal. Place the pastry roll, seam side down, on a baking sheet. Repeat with the remaining squares and chocolate.

3. Brush the tops of the pastry rolls with the remaining egg wash and sprinkle lightly with sugar. Bake until the pastries are golden brown, about 15 minutes. Serve warm or at room temperature.

MAKES 8 PASTRIES

1 sheet frozen puff pastry
(from 17.3-ounce package),
thawed and cut into 8 squares

1 large egg, lightly beaten with
2 teaspoons water

$\frac{1}{2}$ cup chopped bittersweet
chocolate or chocolate chips

Sugar

● cinnamon streusel coffee cake

DON'T YOU LOVE HOW SOME BREAKFAST DISHES are really desserts in disguise? Tina's mother acknowledged the scam and often served the same recipe for a weekend breakfast treat and a speedy evening dessert. This coffee cake has a sugar-cinnamon crumb layer right on top. Enjoy it at any time of the day.

1. Preheat the oven to 350°F. Butter an 8 x 8-inch baking pan and set aside.

2. To prepare the topping: In a small bowl, stir together the flour, brown sugar, and cinnamon. Add the butter and, using a pastry blender or fork, mix the ingredients until the mixture is crumbly and resembles wet sand.

3. To make the cake: In a large bowl, whisk together the flour, sugar, baking powder, and salt. In a medium bowl, whisk together the egg, milk, oil, and vanilla. Pour the wet ingredients into the dry ingredients and stir just to combine. Pour the cake batter into the prepared pan and sprinkle the streusel topping evenly over the batter.

4. Bake for 35 minutes, or until a toothpick inserted in the center comes out clean. Remove from the oven and let cool for at least 15 minutes before cutting into 9 squares. Serve warm or at room temperature.

MAKES 1 (8-INCH) SQUARE COFFEE CAKE; SERVES 9

Topping

$3/4$ cup plus 2 tablespoons all-purpose flour

$1/2$ cup (packed) light brown sugar

1 teaspoon ground cinnamon

5 tablespoons unsalted butter, cut into pieces

Cake

Unsalted butter

$1^1/2$ cups all-purpose flour

$2/3$ cup sugar

2 teaspoons baking powder

$1/4$ teaspoon salt

1 large egg

$1/2$ cup whole milk

$1/3$ cup vegetable oil

1 teaspoon vanilla extract

■ golden granola bars

WE LOVE GRANOLA BARS, but they tend to be expensive and are often packed with hydrogenated oils. We weren't sure how easy it would be to make homemade breakfast squares until we started experimenting. The result is this one-bowl recipe made with real butter and no preservatives. These highly satisfying bars are great at breakfast—or any other time.

1. Preheat the oven to 325°F.

2. Combine the sugar, honey, and butter in a small saucepan. Cook over medium heat until the butter melts and the sugar dissolves.

3. Combine the oats, wheat germ, coconut, almonds, pumpkin seeds, sunflower seeds, and salt in large bowl.

4. Pour the honey mixture over the oat mixture and stir to combine. Spread in a $10^1/_2$ x $15^1/_2$-inch rimmed jelly roll pan and press evenly.

5. Bake for 16 to 18 minutes, or until golden. Cool for 10 minutes before cutting into 25 to 30 bars. Cool completely before removing the bars from the sheet pan.

CHEWY GRANOLA BARS
Use the same ingredients as for Golden Granola Bars plus $^1/_3$ cup golden raisins.

1. Follow the directions for Golden Granola Bars through step 2.

2. Combine the oats, almonds, pumpkin seeds, and sunflower seeds on a baking sheet and toast in the oven for 10 minutes. Remove from the oven and combine with the wheat germ, coconut, salt, and raisins in a large bowl.

3. Pour the honey mixture over the oat mixture and stir to combine. Spread in a $10^1/_2$ x $15^1/_2$-inch rimmed jelly roll pan and press evenly. Cool completely and then refrigerate for at least 1 hour before cutting into bars.

MAKES 25 TO 30 BARS

$^1/_2$ cup (packed) light brown sugar

$^1/_3$ cup honey

6 tablespoons unsalted butter

3 cups old-fashioned rolled oats

$^1/_2$ cup wheat germ

$^1/_3$ cup unsweetened flaked coconut

$^2/_3$ cup sliced almonds

$^1/_3$ cup pumpkin seeds

$^1/_3$ cup sunflower seeds

$^1/_4$ teaspoon salt

almond-cranberry granola

MAKING GRANOLA IS A BIT like tuning your own skis: It takes a little extra effort, but you really know what's been done—and once you try it you'll never pay someone else to do it for you. When this dish is finished baking, you can enjoy it for an entire ski weekend . . . if it lasts that long. As a bonus, you get to put in exactly what you like. We offer two versions here, but clearly the possibilities are endless.

1. Preheat the oven to 325°F.

2. In a large bowl, stir together the oats, almonds, coconut, sunflower seeds, and salt. In a small saucepan over low heat, melt the butter with the honey, stirring to combine. Pour the butter mixture over the oat mixture and stir until thoroughly incorporated.

3. Spread the granola mixture evenly on a large rimmed baking sheet. Bake until golden, 18 to 20 minutes, stirring frequently to prevent overbrowning, particularly near the edges of the baking sheet. Remove from the oven even if the granola doesn't appear crunchy. It will harden as it cools.

4. Cool the granola in the pan for 20 minutes. Stir in the dried cranberries. Store in an airtight container for up to 1 week.

MAKES ABOUT 5 CUPS

3 cups old-fashioned rolled oats

$2/3$ cup sliced almonds

$1/3$ cup slivered almonds

$1/3$ cup unsweetened shredded coconut

$1/4$ cup sunflower seeds

$1/4$ teaspoon salt

3 tablespoons unsalted butter

$1/3$ cup honey

$2/3$ cup dried cranberries

maple-pecan granola

THE NUTS AND MAPLE SYRUP in this second granola version make for a more intense flavor. The coconut takes a backseat here, so if you love coconut, double the amount.

1. Preheat the oven to 325°F.

2. In a large bowl, stir together the oats, pecans, coconut, sunflower seeds, cinnamon, and salt. In a small saucepan over low heat, melt the butter with the maple syrup and sugar, stirring until the sugar is dissolved. Pour the butter mixture over the oat mixture and stir until thoroughly combined.

3. Spread the granola mixture evenly on a large rimmed baking sheet. Bake until golden, about 20 minutes, stirring frequently to prevent overbrowning, particularly near the edges of the baking sheet. Remove from the oven even if the granola doesn't appear crunchy. It will harden as it cools.

4. Cool the granola in the pan for 20 minutes. Stir in the raisins, if desired. Store in an airtight container for up to 1 week.

MAKES ABOUT 5 CUPS

$3^{1}/_{2}$ cups old-fashioned rolled oats

$^{3}/_{4}$ cup chopped pecans

$^{1}/_{3}$ cup unsweetened shredded coconut

$^{1}/_{3}$ cup sunflower seeds

$^{1}/_{2}$ teaspoon ground cinnamon

$^{1}/_{4}$ teaspoon salt

3 tablespoons unsalted butter

$^{1}/_{2}$ cup maple syrup, preferably Grade B

1 tablespoon light brown sugar

$^{2}/_{3}$ cup raisins (optional)

lunch

AFTER THREE HOURS of pointing our skis down the fall line, we are ready to refuel. We're looking for toasty panini or a meaty sandwich. Yet as satisfying as it is to take off the helmet and the gloves at noon, lunch can be the least satisfying meal of a ski trip. Unless you're skiing Deer Valley or one of the handful of other gourmet mountains, the choices are usually overpriced and uninspired. We've had our fill of greasy pizza squares, bland chilis, and scary chowders. What, then, is the answer?

Because we'd rather choose our mountain for the terrain, not for the food, we often bring our own fare, which means it has to tolerate a full morning sitting in the lodge while we bomb down the slopes. Although years of brown bag lunches at school nearly scared us off, we managed to learn a few sandwich tricks in adulthood. We pair our breads and dressings carefully to avoid sogginess. We whip up a version of tuna salad that does not include mayonnaise. We use dense, nutty breads that hold up well for hours. We also diverge from the traditional sandwich layers for a flavorful roast beef wrap that is cut like a sushi roll—easy to make, easy to share.

To transport your lunch to the mountain, we offer a few recommendations. Disposable pie tins are great for inverting over each other and stacking together; we use large rubber bands to secure the impromptu lids. We keep a couple of cool packs in our freezer to tote with cold foods and beverages, but we can always fill sealable baggies with ice cubes in a pinch. We also don't know how we lived without our soft-sided cooler on wheels. Not only does it collapse to stow in the kitchen cupboard, but there's enough room inside for our favorite cooling device of all: a six-pack of ice-cold beer.

Another packing trick we've learned both saves time in the morning and makes for better sandwiches. Instead of assembling sandwiches at home, we often bring our fillings and breads to the mountain and put them together just before eating. Then we can sit down to the freshest meal in the room without missing out on the social phenomenon that lunchtime in the ski lodge provides: the happy din of clomping boots, plastic trays, and lots and lots of bad hairdos.

If we're lucky enough to have ski-on, ski-off accommodations, we can zip home for lunch. A few minutes at the stove produces really gratifying toasted sandwiches—Manchego and Prosciutto Panini, a Colorado Cubano sandwich, or a Croque Monsieur. Or we make calzones in advance and bake them straight from the freezer.

Whichever you choose, after one of these lunches you'll be ready for another three hours or so of vertical drop.

● roast beef–blue cheese roll

THIS IS *THE* SANDWICH to tote to the ski lodge. It won't get soggy. And because it is served in bite-size pieces, it's easy to share with your fellow skiers.

1. Divide the cheese among the tortillas and spread evenly to cover, leaving only 1 inch on the left and the right bare, as those edges will be trimmed off before serving.

2. Starting from the bottom edge of the tortillas, arrange the beef slices in a single layer over the cheese. Sprinkle the parsley on top of the beef, if desired.

3. Starting at the bottom edge, roll tightly upward. The very top of the tortilla should have cheese only as its coating, helping to stick the sandwich together.

4. With a sharp knife, trim off the leftmost and rightmost inch of each tortilla. Cut each sandwich crosswise into $3/4$-inch to 1-inch rounds, like a sushi roll.

SERVES 4

12 ounces semisoft blue cheese, such as domestic Gorgonzola, at room temperature

6 (8- to 10-inch) sandwich wraps or flour tortillas

1 pound thinly sliced roast beef

1 tablespoon chopped fresh parsley (optional)

● hold-the-mayo tuna salad sandwich

UNLIKE THE CLASSIC TUNA SALAD with mayonnaise, this zesty oil-and-vinegar preparation is happy to wait for you in the ski lodge until lunchtime. Now, if only finding a free table were as easy...

1. Mix together the tuna, vinegar, oil, lemon zest, lemon juice, capers, onion, olives, and parsley, if desired, in a medium bowl. Season to taste with salt and pepper.

2. Place the bread slices on a work surface and drizzle lightly with the oil. Layer the tuna salad on 4 of the slices, followed by the avocado and tomato. Top with the remaining slices of bread, oil side down.

NOTE Tuna salad tastes even better if it is refrigerated overnight. Mix it up the night before you plan to eat it for the most delicious sandwich.

SERVES 4

2 (6-ounce) cans tuna packed in olive oil, drained and flaked

1 tablespoon red wine vinegar

1 tablespoon extra-virgin olive oil, plus more for drizzling

1 teaspoon grated lemon zest

2 teaspoons fresh lemon juice

1 tablespoon capers

2 tablespoons diced red onion

2 tablespoons finely chopped kalamata olives

1 tablespoon finely chopped fresh parsley (optional)

Salt and freshly ground black pepper

8 slices seven-grain bread or 1 baguette, cut into 4 pieces, each halved lengthwise

Sliced avocado

Sliced tomato

• turkey, brie, and apple on raisin-walnut bread

THIS TURKEY SANDWICH satisfies cravings for both sweet and savory tastes. It offers contrasting textures as well. The apple stays crisp, and the Brie stays creamy without making the sandwich soggy.

1. In a small bowl, mix together the mustard and honey. Spread the mixture on 4 of the bread slices. Divide the Brie evenly among the remaining 4 slices.

2. Layer the turkey and apple slices on the cheese and top with the remaining slices of bread, honey-mustard side down. Cut in half to serve.

SERVES 4

2 tablespoons Dijon mustard

1 tablespoon honey

8 slices raisin-walnut bread

4 ounces Brie, sliced

8 ounces thinly sliced turkey

1/2 Granny Smith apple, thinly sliced

● not your grandmother's chicken salad

WE'VE NEVER LOVED TRADITIONAL chicken salad because of the excessive mayonnaise and overall lack of flavor. Instead, we like to liven and lighten up cooked chicken with yogurt and herbs. Serve this between two slices of whole-grain bread or over baby greens.

In a large bowl, whisk together the yogurt, mayonnaise, lemon juice, and mustard until blended. Add the chicken, celery, apple, walnuts, and tarragon, if using, and mix thoroughly. Season to taste with salt and pepper. Cover and refrigerate for 1 hour or overnight, to blend the flavors.

SERVES 4

1/3 cup plain nonfat yogurt

1/4 cup mayonnaise

2 tablespoons fresh lemon juice

2 teaspoons Dijon mustard

2 cups (1 pound) diced cooked boneless, skinless chicken breasts

2 celery ribs, diced

1/2 Granny Smith apple, cored and diced

1/3 cup toasted chopped walnuts

3 tablespoons chopped fresh tarragon (optional)

Salt and freshly ground black pepper

■ manchego and prosciutto panini

PANINI ARE GRILLED CHEESE SANDWICHES for grown-ups. They make a quick hot lunch and can accompany nearly any salad or soup. We like this salty, savory sandwich with a bit of sweet quince paste on top.

1. Heat the oil in a large skillet over medium heat.

2. When the oil is hot, place 4 bread slices in the pan. Top each bread slice with a thin layer of prosciutto, then one-quarter of the cheese. Cover with another slice of bread. Using a spatula, carefully flip each sandwich over, then place a slightly smaller skillet on top of the sandwiches. Press down on the top skillet to compress the ingredients and leave it on top as a weight.

3. Cook for 5 to 10 minutes, or until the cheese begins to melt and the bottom piece of bread is brown. Flip and press the sandwiches again, cooking until brown on the second side, about 5 minutes.

4. Remove the sandwiches to a serving plate. Spread a thin layer of membrillo on top of each, if desired. Serve immediately.

SERVES 4

3 tablespoons olive oil

8 slices sourdough sandwich bread

4 ounces Serrano ham, prosciutto, or cooked ham, very thinly sliced

8 ounces manchego cheese, thinly sliced

1 small package membrillo (quince paste), optional

■ colorado cubano

WE LOVE CUBAN SANDWICHES, but sometimes it's not easy to find all of the traditional ingredients in a ski town. Our version takes advantage of widely available deli meats and layers them with Swiss cheese to create a super-hearty sandwich. This satisfying lunch will keep you going, whether you'll be skiing for another three hours or sitting in traffic for four.

---

1. Heat a nonstick griddle, grill pan, or skillet over medium heat. Slice the rolls in half, spread with the mustard, and then add a layer of the cheese to both sides of each roll. Continue building the sandwiches by layering the turkey, ham, and pickles on one side of each roll. Close the sandwiches.

2. Melt the butter on the griddle and add the sandwiches, weighing them down with a heavy skillet. Cook for 3 minutes on each side, pressing down occasionally to flatten, until the bread is crisp and the cheese is melted. Slice in half and serve immediately.

SERVES 4

4 hard rolls, such as kaiser or
   ciabatta

2 tablespoons Dijon mustard

8 ounces sliced Swiss cheese

8 ounces thinly sliced turkey breast

8 ounces thinly sliced smoked ham

4 dill pickles, thinly sliced

2 tablespoons unsalted butter

◆ croque monsieur

ESSENTIALLY A FRENCH GRILLED CHEESE SANDWICH, the Croque Monsieur is a decadent combination of buttered bread, ham, and cheese smothered in béchamel sauce. The calories suggest it's not for every day—but after tackling some serious vertical, you deserve it!

1. Preheat the broiler.

2. To prepare the béchamel: Melt the butter in a small saucepan over medium-low heat. Add the flour and stir for 1 minute. Gradually pour in the milk, whisking constantly. Add the bay leaf. Increase the heat and bring to a boil, stirring frequently, until the sauce thickens, about 2 minutes. Season to taste with salt and pepper, and remove from the heat.

3. To make the sandwiches: Place the bread slices on a work surface. Spread Dijon mustard to taste on 4 of the slices and top with the ham. Sprinkle 2 cups of the Gruyère evenly on top of the ham. Cover with the 4 remaining slices of bread.

4. Heat a large ovenproof skillet over medium heat. Brush the sandwiches on both sides with the melted butter. Cook until the first side is golden, about 3 minutes. Flip the sandwiches and cook for another 3 minutes to brown the other side.

5. Discard the bay leaf and spoon the béchamel sauce over the sandwiches. Top evenly with the remaining 1/2 cup Gruyère. Broil until the cheese is melted and beginning to brown, about 2 minutes. Serve immediately.

SERVES 4

Béchamel

1 tablespoon unsalted butter

1 tablespoon all-purpose flour

2/3 cup whole milk

1 bay leaf

Salt and freshly ground black
    pepper

Sandwiches

8 slices white sandwich bread

Dijon mustard

4 thin slices Black Forest ham

2 1/2 cups grated Gruyère
    (about 10 ounces)

2 tablespoons butter, melted

● black bean quesadillas

WHAT DO YOU TALK ABOUT on the ski lift? Something about being suspended 30 feet in the cold air over glistening snow encourages the discussion of all sorts of unexpected topics. Not long ago we found ourselves discussing the fact that every Western culture has a version of the grilled cheese sandwich. Apparently the combination of bread and cheese has been irresistible to cooks on three continents for generations. You can whip up the Mexican version, a quesadilla, in less time than the high-speed quad can get you to the summit.

SERVES 4 TO 6

Black Bean Dip (page 70) or 2 cups
    store-bought black bean dip

8 (8-inch) flour tortillas

1 cup (4 ounces) shredded
    Monterey Jack

2 cups store-bought guacamole

1 (10-ounce) jar salsa

1. Preheat a large skillet over medium heat. Spread ¼ cup of the black bean dip on half of each tortilla. Top with the shredded cheese and fold over the tortillas to close.

2. Place 4 of the folded tortillas in the skillet and cook until the cheese is melted and the tortillas are lightly browned, about 3 minutes per side. Repeat with the remaining tortillas.

3. Cut the tortillas in half. Serve hot with bowls of guacamole and salsa.

■ sausage, spinach, and ricotta calzones

IF YOUR TOES ARE FROZEN by lunchtime, that's bad—but if your lunch is frozen, that's okay. Assemble a batch of these calzones, wrap them individually, and seal them in a freezer bag, and they'll be perfectly tasty. Simply unwrap the calzones, place them on a baking sheet, and bake straight from the freezer.

1. Preheat the oven to 450°F.

2. Heat the oil in a large skillet over medium-high heat. Add the sausage and cook, breaking up with a wooden spoon, until browned and crumbly, about 5 minutes. Add the garlic and cook for 1 minute more. Remove from the heat and stir in the spinach. Let cool.

3. In a large bowl, stir together the ricotta, mozzarella, Parmesan, salt, and pepper. Add the cooled spinach mixture and stir to combine.

4. Quarter the dough and roll out each piece to an 8-inch round with a rolling pin. Sprinkle lightly with flour if the dough becomes sticky. Place one-fourth of the filling in the center of one dough round and fold in half to form a semicircle. Press the edges together to enclose the filling. Working from one end to the other, fold and pinch the sealed edge over itself to form a ropelike edge. Transfer to a baking sheet and repeat with the remaining dough and filling. (At this point, the calzones can be wrapped and frozen for up to 1 month.)

5. Bake until golden, about 15 minutes. Let cool for 5 minutes before serving. Serve with warm tomato sauce, if desired.

NOTE If baking frozen calzones, heat the oven to 400°F and bake for 40 minutes.

SERVES 4

1 teaspoon olive oil

2 sweet Italian sausage links (about 8 ounces), casings removed

1 garlic clove, minced

1 (10-ounce) package frozen chopped spinach, thawed and squeezed dry

1/2 cup whole-milk ricotta

1 cup (4 ounces) shredded whole-milk mozzarella

3 tablespoons freshly grated Parmesan

1/4 teaspoon salt

1/8 teaspoon freshly ground black pepper

1 pound frozen pizza dough, thawed

Flour

Tomato sauce, warmed (optional)

fifteen-minute stovetop macaroni and cheese

IF YOU HAVE A BLOCK OF CHEDDAR in the fridge and a box of pasta in the pantry, you are just minutes away from a steaming hot bowl of gooey homemade mac and cheese. We make this quick lunchtime version entirely on the stovetop and have been known to scarf it down straight from the pot.

We like sharp Vermont Cheddars for this recipe; our favorite is two-year-old Cheddar, which is flavorful but not so dry that it won't melt smoothly. No matter what cheeses are available in your area, vacuum-packed 8-ounce bars of aged Cheddar seem to keep forever in the refrigerator, so you'll be able to make this recipe whenever hunger strikes.

1. Bring a large pot of salted water to a boil. Add the pasta and cook for 6 minutes.

2. Add the peas to the pasta in the pot and cook for 2 minutes, or until the pasta is al dente and the peas are tender.

3. Reserve 1 cup of the cooking liquid, and then drain the pasta and peas. Return the pasta and peas to the pot and, off the heat, add the butter, stirring with a wooden spoon to coat.

4. Add the cheese in three additions, stirring constantly and drizzling the hot cooking water over the pasta after each addition of cheese as needed. (You may not use all of the water.) Stir until thoroughly combined.

5. Season with salt and pepper to taste. Garnish with the Parmesan and serve immediately.

SERVES 2 TO 4

8 ounces dried elbow macaroni

3/4 cup frozen peas

2 tablespoons unsalted butter

2 cups (8 ounces) shredded sharp Cheddar,

Salt and freshly ground black pepper

Freshly grated Parmesan

soups

COLD WEATHER AND HOT SOUP go together like boots and bindings. On a really cold day, nothing else will do, which is why we have often found ourselves buying steaming cups of soup from whatever remote lodge we happened to find when hunger sets in. We forget that the chowder will likely be floury and bland, and that the chicken noodle will be greasy. Invariably, we are disappointed.

Considering the effort it takes to stock some of the steeper peak lodges—a phalanx of ski bums daily loads food and gear on a Snow-Cat, bumps along at dawn to the peak, unloads the supplies with numb fingers, and assembles everything in a so-called kitchen, all for a free ski pass—we're inclined to forgive these eateries for some of the mediocre fare we've bought there. We realize we are paying for the view and the warmth—the food is incidental.

Luckily, you can prepare many fresh-tasting soups in under an hour and mainly from pantry and freezer items. We freely mix store-bought broths, preferably low-sodium varieties, with lots of fresh ingredients to get a homemade taste without endless simmering and straining. Vegetable soups, in particular, do not benefit from hours of simmering. Make them and enjoy them right away, or freeze them and reheat as needed. Pack hot soup in a thermos for lunch, and you'll be the envy of the lodge.

For a fancier presentation at dinnertime, choose a pureed soup, like the Roasted Butternut Squash Soup, with its brilliant hue, or Creamy Tomato Soup. The prize for the most indulgent recipe in this chapter might go to Classic French Onion Soup, with its cheesy crust, or silky Potato Cheddar Soup.

■ roasted butternut squash soup

THIS SIMPLE SOUP is based on two primary ingredients: butternut squash and garlic. Roasting brings out the flavors in each—so much so that little seasoning is needed to yield a comforting yet elegant soup. If only moguls were so simple.

1. Preheat the oven to 425°F.

2. Generously season the squash with salt and pepper. Place the squash, cut side down, on a rimmed baking sheet. Roast for 35 minutes, or until a knife pierces the squash without resistance. Let cool, and then peel and chop the squash. Set aside.

3. In a large saucepan or stockpot, melt the butter over medium heat. Add the onion and cook until soft, about 6 minutes. Squeeze the roasted garlic into the pot and add the chicken broth and squash. Stir to combine. Bring to a simmer and cook for 5 minutes. Remove from the heat.

4. Using an immersion blender, puree the soup until smooth. Alternatively, transfer the soup in batches to a traditional blender and puree. Taste and adjust the seasoning.

5. Serve immediately; cool, cover, and refrigerate for up to 3 days; or freeze for up to 1 month.

SERVES 6

1 medium butternut squash (about 2$\frac{1}{2}$ pounds), halved lengthwise and seeded

Salt and freshly ground black pepper

2 tablespoons unsalted butter

1 medium yellow onion, diced

1 head Roasted Garlic (page 143)

2$\frac{1}{2}$ cups low-sodium chicken broth

● italian vegetable soup

SHOVE OVER THE VODKA and ice cream in your freezer and make room for leftover Parmesan rinds. Why, might you ask? Because if you keep hard cheese rinds in the freezer, you can create soups with glorious depth of flavor, as in this hearty Italian soup of vegetables, tomatoes, and tiny pasta.

1. Heat the oil in a large pot over medium heat. Add the onion, celery, and carrots and cook until softened, about 8 minutes. Add the garlic and rosemary and cook for 2 minutes more. Squeeze the spinach between your hands to remove any excess moisture before adding it to the pot. Add the pinto and cannellini beans, tomatoes, broth, and Parmesan rind. Stir to combine.

2. Bring the soup to a boil over high heat, and then reduce the heat and simmer for 10 minutes, skimming any foam from the top.

3. Add the pasta and cook until al dente, about 7 minutes. Season generously with pepper and add salt to taste.

4. Serve immediately with grated Parmesan; cool, cover, and refrigerate for up to 3 days; or freeze for up to 1 month.

SERVES 6

2 tablespoons extra-virgin olive oil

1 medium yellow onion, diced

2 celery ribs, diced

2 medium carrots, diced

6 garlic cloves, minced

1 tablespoon finely chopped fresh rosemary or 1 teaspoon dried

1 (10-ounce) package frozen chopped spinach, thawed

1 (15-ounce) can pinto beans, rinsed and drained

1 (15-ounce) can cannellini beans, rinsed and drained

1 (14$\frac{1}{2}$-ounce) can diced tomatoes

5 cups low-sodium chicken broth

1 (3-inch) piece Parmesan rind

1 cup small dried pasta, such as tubetti

Salt and freshly ground black pepper

Freshly grated Parmesan

● broccoli-cauliflower soup

WE LIKE TO RESERVE THE WORD *fatties* to describe our freestyle skis, not our behinds. This soup cooks up fast and is nothing but healthful. We call for a small amount of heavy cream, as it imparts a creamier consistency than a larger amount of milk or half-and-half. The resulting soup is almost completely vegetables, making it a guilt-free warm-up food.

---

1. Heat a large pot over medium heat and melt the butter in it. Add the onions and cook until soft and beginning to brown, about 6 minutes. Add the broccoli, cauliflower, and potatoes. Add the broth and enough water to almost cover the vegetables. Add the salt, and pepper to taste.

2. Bring the soup to a boil and then reduce the heat and simmer for 30 to 35 minutes, or until the vegetables are very tender. Remove from the heat.

3. With an immersion blender, puree the soup until smooth. Alternatively, transfer the soup in batches to a traditional blender and puree. Stir the cream into the hot soup. Taste and adjust the seasonings.

4. Serve immediately; cool, cover, and refrigerate for up to 3 days; or freeze for up to 1 month.

SERVES 6

2 tablespoons unsalted butter

2 medium yellow onions, chopped

1 head broccoli, cut into 2-inch florets, or 1 (16-ounce) package frozen florets

1 head cauliflower, cut into 2-inch florets, or 1 (16-ounce) package frozen florets

1 large or 2 small baking potatoes, peeled and thinly sliced

1 (32-ounce) carton low-sodium chicken broth

$1/2$ teaspoon salt

Freshly ground black pepper

$1/3$ cup heavy cream

● creamy tomato soup

OUR CHILDHOOD SERVINGS of tomato soup came from a can. This version is much yummier, owing to the quick but effective technique of broiling canned whole tomatoes and finishing the soup with a touch of cream. This is the perfect antidote to skiing through cold smoke all day.

1. Preheat the broiler.

2. Strain the tomatoes, reserving the juices. Cut the tomatoes in half lengthwise and spread over a small rimmed baking sheet. Drizzle with 1 tablespoon of the oil and season with salt and pepper. Broil until the tomatoes begin to caramelize, about 10 minutes.

3. In a large pot, heat the remaining 1 tablespoon oil and the butter over medium heat. Add the onion, garlic, and carrot and cook until softened, 7 to 10 minutes. Add the roasted tomatoes, reserved juices, and red pepper flakes and simmer for 15 minutes.

4. Stir in the cream and remove from the heat. Using an immersion blender, puree the soup until smooth. Alternatively, transfer the soup in batches to a traditional blender and puree.

5. Garnish with basil or parsley, if desired, and serve immediately; cool, cover, and refrigerate for up to 3 days; or freeze for up to 1 month.

SERVES 4

1 (28-ounce) can whole peeled tomatoes

2 tablespoons extra-virgin olive oil

Salt and freshly ground black pepper

1 tablespoon unsalted butter

1 medium yellow onion, chopped

3 garlic cloves, minced

1 medium carrot, diced

$1/8$ teaspoon red pepper flakes

$1/3$ cup heavy cream

1 tablespoon chopped fresh basil or parsley (optional)

• potato cheddar soup

THE HEFTY VEGETABLE CONTENT makes this silky homemade soup both healthier and fancier than the pasty restaurant versions we've tasted. This isn't a pureed soup, so you do not need any equipment other than a peeler and a knife, but using a food processor to chop the vegetables and shred the cheese reduces the preparation time to a handful of minutes.

1. Melt the butter in a large pot over medium-high heat until foaming. Add the onion, carrots, celery, and garlic and cook until the vegetables are soft, about 7 minutes. Add the flour and cook, stirring, until the vegetables begin to brown, about 2 minutes.

2. Add the broth, half-and-half, thyme, bay leaf, and potato. Bring the mixture to a boil and then cover and reduce the heat. Simmer until the potato is tender, about 20 minutes. Remove the bay leaf. (The soup can be prepared up to this point, cooled, covered, and refrigerated for up to 3 days, or frozen for up to 1 month. Reheat before proceeding.)

3. Remove from the heat. In handfuls, stir in the cheese until each addition is melted. Serve immediately.

SERVES 4

2 tablespoons unsalted butter

1 large yellow onion, chopped

2 small carrots, chopped

2 small celery ribs, finely chopped

1 large garlic clove, minced

3 tablespoons all-purpose flour

2$1/2$ cups low-sodium chicken broth

2 cups half-and-half or 1 cup milk
  and 1 cup heavy cream

$1/2$ teaspoon dried thyme

1 bay leaf

1 large potato, peeled and diced

2 cups (8 ounces) shredded sharp
  Cheddar

■ white bean with bacon soup

THIS HEARTY SOUP will satisfy even the biggest appetites. Together with crusty bread and a green salad, it makes a midday lunch or a comforting dinner. The bacon makes this otherwise ordinary soup outstanding. What can't it improve?

---

1. In a large pot over medium heat, cook the bacon until crisp, about 8 minutes. Remove the bacon to drain on paper towels.

2. Remove all but 2 tablespoons of the bacon fat from the pot. Add the onion, celery, carrot, shallot, and garlic to the pot and cook for 4 minutes. Add the broth, beans, thyme, and bay leaves and bring to a boil. Reduce the heat and simmer for 15 minutes, or until the beans begin to fall apart.

3. Puree the soup until smooth with an immersion blender. Alternatively, transfer the soup in batches to a traditional blender and puree. Season to taste with salt and pepper.

4. Crumble the reserved bacon. Serve the soup immediately, topped with the bacon.

SERVES 6

5 slices bacon

1 medium yellow onion, diced

1 celery rib, diced

1 medium carrot, diced

1 medium shallot, minced

4 garlic cloves, minced

2½ cups low-sodium chicken broth

2 (15-ounce) cans cannellini or other small white beans

2 sprigs fresh thyme or ½ teaspoon dried

2 bay leaves

Salt and freshly ground black pepper

● super g split pea

THIS STANDBY RECIPE is notable for its simplicity. The ingredients list is limited to pantry staples plus the classic soup vegetables: carrots, onions, and celery. There is no need to drive all over town hunting down odd ingredients! It is also convenient that split peas cook faster than other dried legumes. You can start this soup when the lifts shut down and eat it for supper.

---

1. In a large pot over medium heat, cook the bacon until crisp, about 8 minutes. Remove the bacon to drain on paper towels.

2. Remove all but 2 tablespoons of the bacon fat from the pot. Add the onions, carrots, celery, and garlic and cook for 5 minutes, or until the vegetables begin to soften.

3. Add the split peas, broth, bay leaves, and thyme. Add 2 cups water or as much as is needed to completely cover the vegetables and peas.

4. Return the bacon to the pot and bring to a boil. Cover, reduce the heat, and simmer until the peas are completely softened, about 90 minutes.

5. Remove the bay leaves and puree the soup with an immersion blender. Alternatively, transfer the soup in batches to a traditional blender and puree.

6. Serve immediately, topped with the ham, if desired; cool, cover, and refrigerate for up to 3 days; or freeze for up to 1 month.

SERVES 4

6 slices bacon, chopped

2 medium yellow onions, chopped

2 large or 3 medium carrots, sliced

2 celery ribs, sliced

2 garlic cloves, chopped

3 cups dried split peas

1 (32-ounce) carton low-sodium chicken broth

2 bay leaves

1 tablespoon chopped fresh thyme or 1 teaspoon dried

2 cups cubed ham (optional)

■ curried red lentil soup

IF SPLIT PEAS ARE TOO OLD-SCHOOL for you, try this zippy lentil soup. Its fresh and unexpected flavors work well for lunch on a cold winter's day. You'd never know the ingredients are straight from the pantry.

1. Place the lentils in a large pot with the broth and 3 cups water. Bring to a boil over high heat and then reduce the heat and simmer for 20 minutes.

2. While the lentils are cooking, heat the oil in a medium skillet over medium heat and add the onion, ½ teaspoon of the salt, and the cayenne. Cook until the onion is soft, 6 to 7 minutes. Add the celery, carrots, garlic, cumin, curry powder, and remaining ½ teaspoon salt and cook for 5 minutes. Stir in the ginger and cook for 1 minute more.

3. Add the vegetable mixture to the simmering lentils and cook for 30 minutes.

4. Using an immersion blender, puree the soup until smooth. Alternatively, transfer the soup in batches to a traditional blender and puree. Taste and adjust the seasoning.

5. Serve immediately; cool, cover, and refrigerate for up to 3 days; or freeze for up to 1 month.

SERVES 6

1½ cups dried red lentils, rinsed

3 cups low-sodium chicken broth

2 tablespoons olive oil

1 medium yellow onion, diced

1 teaspoon salt

¼ teaspoon cayenne

2 celery ribs, diced

2 medium carrots, diced

6 garlic cloves, minced

1½ teaspoons cumin

1 teaspoon curry powder

4 teaspoons grated fresh ginger

◆ classic french onion soup

TOO COLD TO STAY OUTSIDE? This recipe requires both time and attention, as well as some fussing at the end with the croutons and melted cheese. But we just can't resist making it—there is almost no more perfect cold weather food. Further, the recipe doesn't require a lot of ingredients, just a little care. There is something magical about producing such complex and indulgent flavor from a pile of onions. It's like making something from nothing.

1. In a large pot, melt 4 tablespoons of the butter over medium heat. Add the onions. Cook, stirring occasionally, for 45 to 60 minutes, or until the onions are deep golden brown. If the onions become dry and begin to stick to the pot before they are nicely browned, add water, 1 tablespoon at a time, to prevent burning.

2. Preheat the oven to 400°F.

3. Add the broth, Cognac (if using), bay leaves, and a pinch of pepper to the pot. Add 1 to 2 cups of water to be sure the onions are covered in liquid. Simmer, uncovered, for 20 minutes.

4. Meanwhile, melt the remaining 2 tablespoons butter in a large skillet over medium-low heat. Add the bread cubes, stir to combine, and toast, stirring as needed, until crisp and lightly browned, about 10 minutes.

5. Remove the bay leaves from the soup and divide the soup among 4 ovenproof bowls. Float the croutons on top and then sprinkle shredded cheese over the croutons. Place the bowls on a baking sheet. Bake for 10 to 15 minutes, or until the cheese is bubbling and beginning to brown. Serve immediately.

SERVES 4

6 tablespoons unsalted butter

6 medium yellow onions, coarsely chopped

4 cups low-sodium beef broth

3 tablespoons Cognac (optional)

2 bay leaves

Freshly ground black pepper

3 cups cubed crusty or stale bread

2 cups (8 ounces) shredded Emmenthaler or other Swiss cheese

après-ski snacks

COMING IN FROM THE COLD is a wonderful feeling. When we finally wrestle off the gear, boots, and gaiters, it can be dangerous to sit down; we might not get up again. Although it is only four o'clock or so, it's already getting dark, and a snack is essential for staving off exhaustion.

Après-ski snacks are all about instant gratification. These recipes are mostly for munchies that take mere minutes to prepare, such as Peppery Popcorn and Mountain Trails Mix. The others are easy to prepare ahead of time, like Sweet and Spicy Glazed Nuts. Have a drink and relax before tackling something as challenging as a shower or setting the table for dinner (see "Beverages," page 17).

Sometimes we find ourselves grazing right into the dinner hour. Why not let your snack turn into a full-blown meal? Fondue makes for a lazy but substantial feast. It can be as simple as cubes of bread dipped into warm cheese and wine, or a more elaborate affair. We include our two favorite varieties: a classically flavored Swiss fondue and our Green Mountain version with aged Cheddar, white wine, and a hint of cayenne.

Whether you require a quick snack on the way to the grocery store or a relaxing drink in front of the fire, taking time to rejuvenate is an essential part of the day.

● kettle corn

BASIC POPCORN IS ONE of the most satisfying snacks you can create in less than ten minutes. But ill-advised technology (like air poppers, which make a Styrofoam-like product) and immediate-gratification products (like microwave bags, which have a zillion milligrams of fat and sodium per serving) have muddled good, wholesome popcorn over the years. We started from scratch to identify the best-tasting recipe for this simple treat. Our version of kettle corn takes away all of the gimmicks. No special equipment is needed, and it tastes great.

MAKES ABOUT 8 CUPS

1 tablespoon peanut or vegetable oil

$^1/_2$ cup popcorn kernels

$1^1/_4$ teaspoons salt

$2^1/_2$ teaspoons sugar

2 tablespoons unsalted butter, melted

1. Heat the oil and 3 popcorn kernels in a large covered pot over medium heat. (A glass lid will let you see what is happening in the pan.)

2. Stir the salt and $1^1/_2$ teaspoons of the sugar together in a small bowl.

3. When the kernels in the pot pop, add the rest of the popcorn. Shake the pan to distribute the kernels in the oil, and set the lid askew by a fraction of an inch. Allowing steam to escape the pan during cooking helps the popcorn develop a crisp texture.

4. After 1 minute has passed but before popping begins, quickly lift the lid and sprinkle the remaining 1 teaspoon sugar over the heating kernels. Shake the pan to distribute the sugar and replace the cover, leaving it slightly askew. Cook until the popping has almost stopped, and then turn off the heat.

5. When all popping has stopped, lift the lid and sprinkle half of the salt mixture over the popped corn, and stir or shake to distribute. Continue to add seasoning until the popcorn is salted to taste.

6. Drizzle the butter over the popcorn, stir, and serve immediately.

☀ PEPPERY POPCORN

Prepare Kettle Corn, omitting the sugar and combining the salt with $^3/_4$ teaspoon ground cumin, $^3/_8$ teaspoon chili powder, and $^1/_8$ teaspoon cayenne.

● spicy roasted chickpeas

WE WERE SERVED A FRIED VERSION of these tasty beans at a bar in Manhattan, alongside overpriced cocktails, and realized that this is the perfect snack to make cocktail hour at home. This unexpected treat is made entirely from pantry staples, and oven-roasting yields the same crunch without the added fat. (See photograph, page 62.)

1. Preheat the oven to 400°F.

2. In a medium bowl, toss the chickpeas with the oil, salt, oregano, garlic powder, and cayenne. Transfer the mixture to a rimmed baking sheet. Bake, stirring the chickpeas every 10 minutes, until golden brown and crisp, about 40 minutes.

3. Transfer the mixture to a bowl and serve warm or at room temperature. These chickpeas are best just after they are prepared, but they will keep in an airtight container for up to 1 day.

MAKES ABOUT 2½ CUPS

2 (15-ounce) cans chickpeas, rinsed, drained, and patted dry

1 tablespoon olive oil

1½ teaspoons salt

1 tablespoon chopped fresh oregano or ¾ teaspoon dried

¼ teaspoon garlic powder

¼ teaspoon cayenne

● mountain trails mix

SOMETIMES WE JUST NEED something in our pocket to munch on the lift, or in the car, or on the way to the car, or . . . Trail mix is the right idea, but commercial mixes always taste stale because dried fruits and nuts aren't meant to be packaged together for any length of time. Dried fruits aren't really dry; they need to retain their moisture to taste fresh. Nuts, on the other hand, taste stale when they become moist. Steer clear of inferior mixes by making your own. Here's our favorite combination of fruit and nuts (and chocolate!), but feel free to be creative.

MAKES 1¹/₂ CUPS

¹/₃ cup pine nuts

¹/₂ cup unsalted roasted almonds

¹/₂ cup dried cranberries

¹/₃ cup semisweet mini chocolate chips (optional)

Salt (optional)

1. In a small pan over medium heat, toast the pine nuts until fragrant and just starting to brown, 3 to 4 minutes. Shake the pan frequently and watch out for burning. Pour onto a plate and set aside to cool completely.

2. Combine the pine nuts with the almonds, cranberries, and chocolate, if using. Salt to taste, if desired. The trail mix is best the day it is made, but it will keep for up to 3 days in an airtight container.

■ sweet and spicy glazed nuts

NUTS ARE THE IDEAL SNACK FOOD because they are healthful, bite-size, shelf-stable, and transportable. Although they are delicious raw, we like to dress them up with this sweet and spicy glaze. Toasting them in the oven intensifies their flavor. Coupled with your favorite après-ski cocktail, these nuts might make it easy to survive a little card game before dinner. (See photograph, page 62.)

1. Preheat the oven to 350°F.

2. In a large skillet over medium heat, warm the butter with the sugar, salt, cumin, cayenne, and 1 tablespoon water. Stir until the butter is melted and the sugar is dissolved, about 2 minutes. Add the nuts and continue to cook, stirring frequently, for 5 more minutes.

3. Spread the nuts on a rimmed baking sheet in a single layer. Bake for 10 minutes, stirring once halfway through, until fragrant and golden.

4. Remove from the oven and cool completely before serving or storing. The nuts can be stored in an airtight container for up to 5 days.

MAKES 3½ CUPS

2 tablespoons unsalted butter

⅓ cup (packed) dark brown sugar

1 teaspoon salt

½ teaspoon ground cumin

½ teaspoon cayenne

3½ cups unsalted mixed nuts, such as pecans, walnuts, and almonds

● baked spinach and artichoke dip

TINA'S SISTER IS KNOWN far and wide for her baked artichoke dip. We love it too, even if she is a snowboarder. We took the basic recipe and added frozen spinach for a heartier mixture. Although the ingredients list looks a tad long, the recipe instructions are essentially "stir together and bake until bubbly." We love that.

Preheat the oven to 350°F. In a shallow 2-quart baking dish, combine the artichokes, spinach, sour cream, mayonnaise, lemon juice, garlic, Parmesan, salt, and cayenne. Stir to thoroughly combine. Top with the cheese. Bake for 25 minutes until bubbly and beginning to brown. Serve with chips or crackers.

MAKES ABOUT 2^1/$_2$ CUPS

1 (13^3/$_4$-ounce) can artichokes packed in water, drained and chopped

1 (10-ounce) package frozen spinach, thawed and squeezed dry

^{1}/$_3$ cup sour cream

^{1}/$_3$ cup mayonnaise

1 teaspoon fresh lemon juice

1 garlic clove, minced

^{2}/$_3$ cup freshly grated Parmesan

^{1}/$_4$ teaspoon salt

^{1}/$_8$ teaspoon cayenne

^{1}/$_2$ cup shredded Monterey Jack

Pita chips, tortilla chips, or assorted crackers

freezer trouble?

YOU WALK INTO YOUR SKI HOUSE, and all the clocks are blinking. The power has gone out since you were last there. Those winds that bring the powder to your doorstep also occasionally knock over a wire somewhere. You've got candles and flashlights—you're ready. There's just one question: Are those frozen calzones in the freezer still good? Should you throw away the brisket?

Late-model freezers do a remarkable insulation job; it would be quite a long blackout indeed that thawed everything in there, especially if nobody was around to open the door. But it's better to be safe than sorry, so you want to be sure you're eating food that has remained properly frozen. Defrosted meats allow bacteria to flourish.

Luckily, there is a simple way to tell at a glance whether frozen food has suffered. Store your ice cubes in a bin inside the freezer instead of in the ice cube trays. Not only will this technique speed the cocktail-making process, you'll also have a clue to your freezer's recent history. If the cubes are loose in the bin when you return, no defrosting occurred. If they stick together just a tiny bit, things are probably still fine, though you should plan on cooking meats and other perishables sooner rather than later. If a puddle has had a chance to form on the bottom of the ice cube bin and then refreeze into a solid mass, some serious defrosting has occurred. Proceed with caution, and throw away questionable foods.

■ back bowl bagna cauda (warmed olive oil dip)

THE ITALIAN VERSION OF FONDUE, bagna cauda is an intensely flavored, warm olive oil made for dipping; vegetables and bread are the perfect vehicles for its zestiness. It is perfect as a festive appetizer for a crowd.

1. Heat $\frac{1}{4}$ cup of the oil in a medium saucepan over low heat. Add the garlic, anchovies, red pepper flakes, and butter and cook until the butter is melted and the anchovies are broken down, about 4 minutes.

2. Add the lemon juice, remaining $\frac{3}{4}$ cup oil, salt, and pepper. Gently simmer for 2 minutes.

3. Transfer the mixture to a fondue pot or warmed bowl. Serve with assorted vegetables and bread for dipping.

MAKES ABOUT 1$\frac{1}{2}$ CUPS

1 cup extra-virgin olive oil

8 garlic cloves, minced

10 anchovies, chopped (rinsed first if packed in salt)

$\frac{1}{4}$ teaspoon red pepper flakes

4 tablespoons ($\frac{1}{2}$ stick) unsalted butter

$\frac{1}{2}$ teaspoon fresh lemon juice

$\frac{1}{2}$ teaspoon salt

$\frac{1}{4}$ teaspoon freshly ground black pepper

Steamed asparagus, carrots, and red pepper strips

Blanched broccoli

Cubed bread

● black bean dip

THIS DIP IS TASTIER AND HEALTHIER than any version from a can, and with the exception of the lime and cilantro, all of the ingredients are straight from the pantry. Top the dip with shredded Cheddar or Jack cheese, heat until bubbly, and serve with chips. It also makes a great filling for quesadillas.

---

1. Place the garlic, lime juice, and oil in a food processor and process until the garlic is chopped finely. Add the beans, cumin, coriander, cayenne, salt, and pepper. Puree until smooth. Alternatively, mince the garlic by hand and mash everything together with a fork. The dip will have more texture but will still taste great.

2. Add the reserved bean liquid as necessary to reach the desired consistency. Transfer the bean dip to a bowl and stir in the cilantro, if desired. Serve with tortilla chips for dipping.

MAKES ABOUT 2 CUPS

2 garlic cloves

2 tablespoons fresh lime juice

1 tablespoon olive oil

1 (15-ounce) can black beans, drained, liquid reserved

3/4 teaspoon ground cumin

1/2 teaspoon ground coriander

1/8 teaspoon cayenne

1/2 teaspoon salt

1/4 teaspoon freshly ground black pepper

1 tablespoon chopped fresh cilantro (optional)

Tortilla chips

roasted red pepper, feta, and white bean dip

ALTHOUGH MADE FROM MOSTLY pantry ingredients, this dip has a nice, fresh taste, courtesy of the feta cheese. You'll need a food processor, but you won't need to slave over a hot stove.

1. Combine the beans, peppers, lemon juice, garlic, oil, cayenne, salt, and pepper in the bowl of a food processor fitted with a metal blade. Process until smooth.

2. Add the feta and oregano and pulse to just combine. Transfer the contents to a small bowl.

3. Serve with toasted pita wedges. The dip can be covered and refrigerated for up to 3 days.

MAKES ABOUT 2 CUPS

1 (15-ounce) can cannellini beans, rinsed and drained

$\frac{1}{2}$ cup roasted red peppers, drained and roughly chopped

3 tablespoons fresh lemon juice

2 garlic cloves, roughly chopped

2 tablespoons extra-virgin olive oil

$\frac{1}{2}$ teaspoon cayenne

$\frac{1}{2}$ teaspoon salt

$\frac{1}{2}$ teaspoon freshly ground black pepper

1 cup (4 ounces) crumbled feta

1 tablespoon chopped fresh oregano or 1 teaspoon dried

Pita bread, cut into triangles

■ classic swiss fondue

YOU CAN SERVE THIS CHEESY GOODNESS simply, with just bread, or turn it into your evening meal with meats and vegetables. Fondue took off in the United States in the 1970s, and Tina's family spent many an evening gathered around little fondue pots, building a meal piece by piece. Though we've put our bell bottoms away, fondue is still perfect after a day on the slopes, when you feel the need to spin tall tales of the big air you caught—sure you did! This is the classic Swiss version, minus the kirsch, which we never seem to have on hand. If you do, and you miss it in this recipe, you can add one to two tablespoons to taste when you add the wine.

1. In a large bowl, toss the Gruyère, Emmenthaler, and Comté with the cornstarch until well combined.

2. Rub the inside of a heavy medium saucepan and a fondue pot with the garlic; discard the garlic. Place the saucepan over medium heat, add the wine and lemon juice, and bring to a simmer. Remove the pan from the heat. Gradually add the cheese mixture to the saucepan, one handful at a time, stirring after each addition until the cheese is melted.

3. Transfer the mixture to the fondue pot and place it on its stand over a low flame. Serve immediately with fondue forks and with cubed bread, vegetables, or meat for dipping.

SERVES 4 TO 6

2 cups (8 ounces) grated Gruyère

2 cups (8 ounces) grated Emmenthaler

2 cups (8 ounces) grated Comté

1 tablespoon cornstarch

1 garlic clove, halved

1¼ cups dry white wine

1 teaspoon fresh lemon juice

Cubed bread; steamed or roasted vegetables, such as broccoli, cauliflower, asparagus, or small potatoes; or cubed cooked meats, including chicken and beef

■ green mountain fondue

ALTHOUGH TRADITIONALISTS MAY BLANCH at the thought, Cheddar makes a terrific fondue. The bold flavor of the cheese takes well to a hint of cayenne. Might as well go for a little spice in life.

---

1. Crush each garlic clove with the blade of a chef's knife, then peel and cut in half. Rub the inside of a fondue pot with the garlic and then leave it in the bottom of the pot.

2. Pour the wine into a medium saucepan and bring to a simmer over medium heat. Add the cornstarch and whisk until smooth.

3. Begin adding the Monterey Jack to the wine mixture, one small handful at a time, whisking until smooth. When half of the Monterey Jack is melted, begin adding the Cheddar in the same way, until half is absorbed. Then alternate between the cheeses until all is melted. Stir in the cayenne.

4. Transfer the mixture to the fondue pot. Serve immediately over a low flame, with fondue forks and bread, vegetables, or meat for dipping.

SERVES 6

4 garlic cloves

1 cup dry white wine

1 teaspoon cornstarch

3 cups (12 ounces) shredded Monterey Jack

3 cups (12 ounces) shredded sharp Cheddar

1/8 teaspoon cayenne

Cubed bread; steamed or roasted vegetables, such as broccoli, cauliflower, asparagus, or small potatoes; or cubed cooked meats, including chicken and beef

pastas

OUR FRIENDS WHO WORKED for a while as lifties never were paid very well, but the job had serious perks, including unlimited free skiing on some great Western mountains. Pasta was their official food; it is quick to prepare, inexpensive, and quite scalable—it is nearly as easy to make pasta for eight people as for two.

We've all turned to pasta for quick sustenance as well as for comfort, and a can of chopped tomatoes in the cupboard means you're never far from a fast meal. However, to make sure we're preparing something fresh and interesting, many of the recipes in this chapter do not involve tomatoes. That doesn't mean they aren't convenient, however; many of the sauces can be prepared while the pasta is cooking, like the butter and sage for ravioli, the carbonara, and the creamy pumpkin.

Just because pasta is quick doesn't mean it can't be indulgent. For creamy richness, we like Baked Macaroni and Cheese and Schuss Shells (Pasta with Gorgonzola Cream Sauce).

You might notice that there aren't any black diamond recipes in this chapter, and few intermediates. We view pasta as the easy way down the mountain—you know the trails we mean, the ones that wind past all the condos. So slow down and enjoy the view. Pair any of these dishes with a salad and a glass of wine, and sit right down to a complete meal.

■ off-piste orecchiette with sausage and broccoli rabe

IF YOU THINK GROOMERS ARE BORING, you probably do a lot of skiing off-piste. If you're used to thinking of pasta as ho-hum, try this recipe. The classic combination of sausage and broccoli rabe will have you loading up on seconds.

1. Bring a large pot of salted water to a boil, add the orecchiette, and cook for 9 to 11 minutes, or until not quite al dente.

2. Meanwhile, heat the oil in a large skillet over medium heat. Add the sausage and cook, breaking it up with a spoon, until browned, about 5 minutes. Add the garlic and red pepper flakes and cook for 1 minute more.

3. Add the broth and broccoli rabe and cook, covered, until the broccoli rabe is tender, about 4 minutes. Drain the pasta, transfer to the skillet, and cook for 1 minute, stirring thoroughly to combine.

4. Season with salt and pepper and serve immediately, topped with the Parmesan.

SERVES 4 TO 6

1 pound dried orecchiette

3 tablespoons extra-virgin olive oil

12 ounces sweet Italian pork sausage (about 3 links), casings removed

4 garlic cloves, minced

$\frac{1}{4}$ teaspoon red pepper flakes

$\frac{1}{2}$ cup low-sodium chicken broth

1 large bunch broccoli rabe, stems trimmed, chopped

Salt and freshly ground black pepper

$\frac{1}{4}$ cup freshly grated Parmesan

■ baked macaroni and cheese

YOU MAY HAVE GROWN UP loving commercial boxed macaroni and cheese, but there's nothing quite like the experience of eating the homemade version. This is the ultimate comfort food to warm you after hours in 30°F weather.

1. Preheat the oven to 375°F. Butter a 9 x 13-inch baking dish and set aside. Bring a large pot of salted water to a boil.

2. Melt the 4 tablespoons butter in a large saucepan over medium heat. Whisk in the flour and cook for 1 minute, stirring frequently. Slowly pour in the milk, whisking constantly until smooth. Bring to a boil, then reduce the heat to medium-low and simmer for 3 minutes, or until the sauce is thickened.

3. Remove from the heat and add 2 cups of the Cheddar and 1 cup of the Monterey Jack; stir until melted. Add the mustard, cayenne, and salt and pepper to taste.

4. Meanwhile, add the pasta to the boiling water and cook for 10 to 12 minutes, or until al dente. Drain the pasta thoroughly and return it to the pot. Add the cheese sauce and stir until combined. Spread the pasta mixture in the prepared baking dish. Sprinkle the remaining 1 cup Cheddar and 1 cup Monterey Jack evenly over the top.

5. Bake for 30 minutes, or until bubbling and golden on top. Let stand for 15 minutes before serving.

NOTE This recipe can be made ahead through step 4 and then wrapped tightly and refrigerated for up to 24 hours before baking.

SERVES 4 TO 6

4 tablespoons (½ stick) unsalted butter, plus more for the baking dish

¼ cup all-purpose flour

1 quart whole milk

3 cups (12 ounces) shredded sharp Cheddar

2 cups (8 ounces) shredded Monterey Jack

1 tablespoon Dijon mustard

¼ teaspoon cayenne

Salt and freshly ground black pepper

1 pound dried pasta, such as macaroni or penne

● spaghetti carbonara

THIS CLASSIC ITALIAN BACON-AND-EGGS pasta dish is also a delicious pantry-and-fridge staples recipe. With just a few ingredients that you might normally eat for breakfast, you can whip up a satisfying dinner in less time than it takes to make it through the lift line on Presidents' Day weekend.

1. Bring a large pot of salted water to a boil. Add the pasta and cook for 10 to 12 minutes, or until al dente.

2. While the pasta is cooking, heat a large skillet over medium-high heat. Add the pancetta and cook until crisp, about 6 minutes. Remove all but 1 tablespoon of the fat.

3. Reserve ¹/₂ cup of the pasta water and then drain the pasta. Add the pasta to the skillet of pancetta and toss to combine.

4. In a large bowl, whisk the eggs with the egg yolks. Turn off the heat under the skillet, add the eggs and 1 cup of the cheese, and toss thoroughly to combine. Add the reserved pasta water as needed to thin the sauce to the desired consistency. Generously season with pepper and add salt to taste.

5. Serve immediately with the remaining ¹/₄ cup cheese sprinkled on top.

SERVES 4 TO 6

1 pound dried spaghetti

8 ounces pancetta or 8 slices thick-cut bacon, diced

2 large eggs

2 large egg yolks

1¹/₄ cups (5 ounces) freshly grated Pecorino Romano

Salt and freshly ground black pepper

● bow ties with salmon

MAKE THIS VERSATILE PASTA with leftover roasted salmon, canned salmon, or even smoked salmon. We admit that we've also made it after casually inviting a crowd for dinner and then realizing we didn't have enough salmon to serve on its own. In any case, serve it with a glass of chardonnay and a salad, and your guests will think you're a hero.

---

1. Bring a large pot of salted water to a boil. Add the pasta and cook until al dente, about 10 minutes.

2. Meanwhile, in a large skillet, heat the oil and garlic over medium-high heat until the garlic just begins to brown, about 3 minutes. Add the tomatoes and a pinch of salt. Bring to a boil, reduce the heat to medium-low, and simmer until the tomatoes are reduced, about 5 minutes.

3. Add the salmon, cream, and a pinch of salt to the tomato mixture. Cook over medium-high heat until reduced slightly, about 4 minutes. Taste and adjust the seasoning.

4. Drain the pasta and add it to the sauce. Toss thoroughly and serve immediately with pepper.

SERVES 4 TO 6

1 pound dried farfalle

2 tablespoons extra-virgin olive oil

1 garlic clove, minced

1 (14-ounce) can whole peeled tomatoes, drained and chopped

Salt

2 cups cooked salmon or 2 (7^1/$_2$-ounce) cans

1 cup heavy cream

Freshly ground black pepper

● schuss shells
(pasta with gorgonzola cream sauce)

THIS IS ONE OF THE CREAMIEST, richest, most indulgent recipes in our repertoire. Blue cheese, heavy cream, and butter are ingredients that alone are luxurious—combined as a pasta sauce, they're heavenly. Needless to say, we feel we can eat it only after some serious schussing. This incredibly simple yet elegant dish can be a special-occasion first course, a main course, or even a side dish served with a roast.

---

1. Bring a large pot of salted water to a boil. Add the pasta and cook for 9 to 11 minutes, or until al dente.

2. While the pasta is cooking, melt the butter and Gorgonzola in a large skillet over low heat. Cook, stirring frequently, until the cheese is melted and the sauce is creamy, about 5 minutes. Add the heavy cream and cook over medium heat until the sauce is thickened and reduced slightly, 3 to 4 minutes. Adjust the seasoning with salt and pepper to taste.

3. Drain the pasta and transfer to the skillet with the cheese sauce. Add the Parmesan and toss thoroughly to coat. Serve immediately with additional pepper.

SERVES 4 TO 6

1 pound dried pasta shells

2 tablespoons unsalted butter

4 ounces Gorgonzola, crumbled (about 1 cup)

$1/2$ cup heavy cream

Salt and freshly ground black pepper

$1/4$ cup freshly grated Parmesan

penne alla vodka

WHAT'S A SKI HOUSE without a bottle of vodka kicking around? Stop mixing cocktails long enough to try this delicious sauce. You may already have all the ingredients on hand! (We're the kind of people who stock both vodka and heavy cream, but that might just be us.)

1. Bring a large pot of salted water to a boil.

2. Meanwhile, heat the oil and garlic in a large saucepan over medium heat. Cook for 2 minutes. Add the tomatoes, vodka, and a pinch of salt and cook until reduced, about 20 minutes.

3. Add the pasta to the boiling water and cook until al dente, about 10 minutes.

4. Add the cream to the tomato mixture and cook for 5 minutes. Taste for seasoning, adding salt and pepper as needed.

5. Drain the pasta, transfer to the saucepan, and toss with the vodka sauce. Serve immediately, topped with pepper and Parmesan.

SERVES 4 TO 6

2 tablespoons extra-virgin olive oil

2 garlic cloves, minced

1 (28-ounce) can whole peeled tomatoes, with juice, chopped

1/2 cup vodka

Salt

1 pound dried penne

2/3 cup heavy cream

Freshly ground black pepper

Freshly grated Parmesan

● creamed spinach fettuccine

WE ADMIT IT: We never order fettuccine Alfredo in a restaurant because we're sure the fat and calories will top out at an unspeakable number. We don't have the same hang-up about creamed spinach, however, because everyone knows spinach is good for you. Here is a pasta that combines the best of both worlds.

1. Bring a large pot of salted water to a boil, add the pasta, and cook according to package directions until al dente.

2. Meanwhile, melt the butter in a large skillet over medium heat. Add the spinach and cream and cook, stirring frequently, until the cream is reduced, about 8 minutes. Season with the nutmeg, salt, and pepper.

3. Drain the pasta and add it to the spinach in the skillet. Add 1 cup of the Parmesan and toss thoroughly to coat. Serve immediately, topped with the remaining 1/4 cup Parmesan.

MAKES 4 TO 6 SERVINGS

1 pound fresh or dried fettuccine, preferably spinach fettuccine

5 tablespoons unsalted butter

1 (10-ounce) package frozen chopped spinach, thawed, excess water squeezed out

1 1/4 cups heavy cream

Pinch of ground nutmeg

Salt and freshly ground black pepper

1 1/4 cups freshly grated Parmesan

rigatoni with sausage and ricotta

WE LIKE TO THINK OF THIS DISH as a stovetop version of lasagne. Italian sausage gives the piquant sauce depth of flavor, while the ricotta adds a touch of creaminess without making it too rich. The result is a simple, sophisticated meal.

1. Bring a large pot of salted water to a boil. Add the pasta and cook until al dente, about 12 minutes.

2. Meanwhile, heat the oil in a large skillet over medium heat. Add the sausage and cook, breaking it up with a spoon, until browned, about 5 minutes. Stir in the tomato sauce and ricotta and cook for 3 minutes more, or until bubbling. Taste and adjust the seasoning with salt and pepper as needed.

3. Drain the pasta, transfer to the skillet, and toss to combine. Serve immediately, topped with the Parmesan.

SERVES 4 TO 6

1 pound dried rigatoni

1 tablespoon extra-virgin olive oil

12 ounces sweet Italian pork sausage (about 3 links), casings removed

1 (25-ounce) jar tomato sauce or Buttery Tomato Sauce (page 93)

1/2 cup ricotta

Salt and freshly ground black pepper

1/4 cup freshly grated Parmesan

■ baked manicotti

WE NEVER USED TO USE those stick-on foot warmers in our boots. Now we realize they provide a big payoff for just a little extra preparation. We feel the same way about homemade manicotti. The preparation is much quicker than that of many baked pastas, yet the result is very satisfying.

1. Preheat the oven to 350°F.

2. Bring a large pot of salted water to a boil. Add the pasta and cook for 5 minutes or until not quite al dente. Drain and toss with the olive oil to prevent sticking. Set aside.

3. Meanwhile, in a medium bowl, stir together the ricotta, 1 cup of the Parmesan, $1/2$ cup of the mozzarella, the egg, garlic, herbs (if using), salt, and pepper.

4. Cover the bottom of a 9 x 13-inch baking dish with 1 cup of the tomato sauce. Spoon the cheese mixture evenly into the manicotti shells and place them in the baking dish. Cover with the remaining 2 cups sauce. Top with the remaining $1/2$ cup mozzarella and $1/4$ cup Parmesan. Cover with aluminum foil.

5. Bake for 30 minutes, remove the foil, and bake for 10 more minutes, or until the cheese is melted and bubbling. Serve immediately.

NOTE The recipe can be made ahead through step 4 and then wrapped tightly and refrigerated for up to 24 hours before baking.

SERVES 4

8 manicotti shells

1 tablespoon olive oil

$1^2/_3$ cups ricotta

$1^1/_4$ cups (5 ounces) freshly grated Parmesan

1 cup (4 ounces) shredded mozzarella

1 large egg

1 garlic clove, minced

1 tablespoon chopped fresh parsley (optional)

1 tablespoon chopped fresh basil (optional)

$1/2$ teaspoon salt

$1/4$ teaspoon freshly ground black pepper

1 (25-ounce) jar tomato sauce or Buttery Tomato Sauce (page 93)

pasta with creamy pumpkin sauce

DID YOU EVER THINK there *must* be more to do with a can of pumpkin puree than make pie? This pasta sauce is your answer. With just a few wintertime ingredients, you can turn the ever-popular pumpkin-filled ravioli inside out.

1. Bring a large pot of salted water to a boil.

2. Melt the butter in a large skillet over medium heat. Add the shallot and garlic and cook for 3 minutes. Add the pumpkin, broth, cream, and half of the sage. Cook, stirring frequently, for about 10 minutes, or until slightly thickened. Season to taste with salt and pepper and stir to combine.

3. Meanwhile, cook the pasta in the boiling water for about 10 minutes, or until al dente. Drain well and add to the pumpkin sauce along with 1/4 cup of the Parmesan.

4. Serve immediately, topped with the remaining 1/4 cup Parmesan and the remaining sage.

SERVES 4 TO 6

1 tablespoon unsalted butter

1 medium shallot, minced, or 2 tablespoons finely chopped onion

3 garlic cloves, minced

3/4 cup canned unsweetened pumpkin puree

3/4 cup low-sodium chicken broth

1/2 cup heavy cream

2 tablespoons chopped fresh sage leaves or 2 teaspoons dried

Salt and freshly ground black pepper

1 pound dried pasta, such as penne or rigatoni

1/2 cup freshly grated Parmesan

■ penne with asparagus in lemon butter sauce

ASPARAGUS IS AN EARLY SPRING CROP, at its best before the snow melts in the mountains. The tender stalks are available locally before spring skiing days arrive. We roast them and then dress them up with pantry ingredients for one of our favorite pasta preparations.

---

1. Preheat the oven to 400°F. Bring a large pot of salted water to a boil.

2. Spread the pine nuts on a baking sheet and toast in the oven for 4 minutes, shaking once after 2 minutes. Check the color of the nuts often, as they burn easily. Set the toasted nuts aside.

3. Trim the woodiest portion at the bottom of each stalk of asparagus. Peel thick spears at the bottom with a vegetable peeler to remove excess fibrous threads. Cut the spears crosswise into 2-inch sections. Place the asparagus on a baking sheet, drizzle with the oil, and toss to coat. Season with salt and pepper. Roast in the oven for 8 to 12 minutes, or until fork tender and beginning to brown.

4. Meanwhile, cook the pasta in the boiling water for about 10 minutes, or until just al dente.

5. Drain the pasta and return it to the pot, along with the lemon juice and broth. Stir over medium heat until slightly thickened, about 5 minutes. Add the butter and stir until melted. Stir in ½ cup of the Parmesan, the asparagus, the pine nuts, and pepper to taste.

6. Serve immediately, sprinkled with the remaining ¼ cup Parmesan.

SERVES 4 TO 6

⅓ cup pine nuts

1 bunch asparagus (1 to 1½ pounds)

3 tablespoons olive oil

Salt and freshly ground black pepper

1 pound dried penne

¼ cup plus 2 teaspoons lemon juice

2 cups low-sodium chicken broth

4 tablespoons (½ stick) unsalted butter

¾ cup freshly grated Parmesan

• ravioli with sage butter sauce

HAVE YOU EVER MADE YOUR OWN RAVIOLI? It's a bit like attempting the half-pipe: Eventually you'll make it down, but the trip might be a bit sloppy. We take the easy way out; prepared commercial ravioli is a trump card to have stashed in the freezer. It's hearty and cooks up in minutes. Although ravioli is lovely served with tomato sauce, we prefer this savory combination of browned butter, sage, and walnuts.

1. Bring a large pot of salted water to a boil. Add the ravioli and cook until al dente, 7 to 9 minutes for frozen, 3 to 4 for fresh.

2. Meanwhile, melt the butter in a large skillet over medium-high heat. Cook until lightly browned, about 5 minutes. Stir in the walnuts and chopped sage and cook for 1 minute. Season with a pinch of salt and pepper and remove from the heat.

3. Drain the pasta and transfer to a large platter. Pour the butter sauce over the pasta and top with the Parmesan. Toss thoroughly to coat. Serve immediately, topped with pepper and the whole sage leaves, if desired.

SERVES 4

1 pound fresh or frozen ravioli

5 tablespoons unsalted butter, cut into pieces

1/4 cup chopped walnuts

1 tablespoon chopped fresh sage leaves or 1 teaspoon dried, plus 4 whole leaves for garnish (optional)

Salt and freshly ground black pepper

1/4 cup freshly grated Parmesan

freeze ahead

THE FOLLOWING RULE has broad applications in the kitchen: *Never make just one lasagne.* Sometimes we find that we don't make our favorite dishes as often as we'd like to enjoy them. They may require a lot of hands-on preparation, like enchiladas, or be messy, like meatballs. No matter. If you make a double recipe of these foods each time you prepare them, the requisite fuss or mess will be even more worthwhile, since you'll get as your reward an entirely fuss-free, mess-free second meal.

Of course, you can get frozen prepared food at the grocery store—but it almost always contains tons of sodium and tastes processed. We stick to the ice cream section of the frozen foods aisle and make our entrées at home. When you're hungry, fewer sights are more gratifying than a freezer containing two or three pre-made meals. Tuck one into the oven and defrost *yourself* while your meal cooks. In about an hour, you'll be sitting down to dinner.

To avoid tying up your casserole dishes in the freezer, line the dish with plastic wrap before you fill it. When the food has frozen completely, remove the casserole from the freezer and slide the contents from the dish. Rewrap completely in plastic wrap and store inside a labeled plastic bag. Before cooking the meal, unwrap and replace the food in the dish.

To avoid discovering a cold spot in the middle of your dinner, be sure that pan sauces are avidly bubbling and browning has begun before removing the baked meal from the oven. Finally, stick a metal knife into the center and leave it there for a minute. Remove it and carefully put it near your lips. It should be hot, not cold or room temperature.

■ meatballs

SOMEHOW, PLAIN SPAGHETTI with sauce feels like a meager meal, while spaghetti with meatballs is always a party. By making this recipe ahead and freezing it, you can decide to serve the meatballs all at once to four very hungry adults or remove them a few at a time for emergency meals. They reheat easily on the stovetop while partially submerged in your favorite tomato sauce. These are traditionally beefy meatballs; serve them with pasta or spoon them onto sandwich rolls for the kind of meal that can't be called anything but *hearty*.

1. Place the bread crumbs in a large bowl, pour the milk over them, stir, and set aside to soak for 5 minutes.

2. Add the beef, pork, Parmesan, egg, onion, garlic, and parsley, if using, to the bowl. Season with salt and pepper and mix with your hands. Form the mixture into 1^1/$_2$-inch balls.

3. Heat the oil in a large skillet over medium-high heat. When the skillet is very hot, add half of the meatballs to the pan. Do not touch them for at least 3 minutes. Turn the meatballs and continue to cook, turning as needed, until they are well browned and cooked through. Each batch may take up to 20 minutes to cook. The meatballs are done when the internal temperature reaches 145°F, as measured on an instant-read thermometer.

4. Serve immediately, or freeze the meatballs on a tray covered with plastic wrap for 1 hour, before transferring them to a freezer bag.

MAKES 28 (1^1/$_2$-INCH)
MEATBALLS; SERVES 4 TO 6

1 cup fresh bread crumbs

1 cup whole milk

1 pound ground beef

8 ounces ground pork

^{3}/$_4$ cup grated Parmesan

1 large egg

^{1}/$_2$ medium yellow onion, finely chopped

1 large garlic clove, minced

3 tablespoons finely chopped fresh parsley (optional)

Salt and freshly ground black pepper

2 tablespoons vegetable oil

■ hearty lasagne

THIS MEATY LASAGNE can be made ahead of time and frozen. All it needs is about an hour in the oven to emerge bubbly and delicious.

1. Bring a large pot of salted water to a boil. Add the lasagna noodles and cook until just tender, about 10 minutes. Drain thoroughly and toss with a little oil to prevent sticking. Set aside.

2. Heat 1 tablespoon oil in a large skillet over medium-high heat. Add the beef and sausage and cook, breaking the meat into small pieces, until browned and no pink remains, about 12 minutes. Add the garlic and oregano and cook for 1 minute. Remove from the heat, drain off the fat, and stir in the tomato paste. Set aside to cool.

3. Preheat the oven to 375°F.

4. In a large bowl, combine the ricotta, parsley (if using), eggs, and ½ cup of the Parmesan. Season with salt and pepper.

5. Coat the bottom of a 9 x 13-inch baking dish with 1 cup tomato sauce. Layer with 4 overlapping noodles. Spread half of the meat mixture over the pasta and spread half of the ricotta mixture on top. Reserve 1 cup mozzarella before sprinkling half of the remaining cheese over the ricotta. Top with 1½ cups tomato sauce, spreading evenly. Repeat with the next layer of noodles, meat, cheeses, and sauce. Top the last layer with noodles and sauce and then sprinkle with the reserved 1 cup mozzarella and ½ cup Parmesan. Wrap tightly in aluminum foil. At this point, the lasagne can be frozen for up to 2 months.

6. Bake for 50 minutes. Remove the foil and bake for 10 minutes more, or until the top is golden and the filling is bubbling.

7. Remove from the oven and let the lasagne rest for 10 to 20 minutes before cutting and serving.

NOTE Bake frozen lasagne at 375°F for 1 hour before removing the foil.

SERVES 10 TO 12

1 pound dried lasagna noodles

Olive oil

1 pound ground beef

12 ounces sweet Italian pork sausage (about 3 links), casings removed

2 garlic cloves, minced

¾ teaspoon dried oregano

1 (6-ounce) can tomato paste

1 (32-ounce) container ricotta

¼ cup chopped fresh parsley (optional)

2 large eggs, lightly beaten

1 cup freshly grated Parmesan

Salt and freshly ground black pepper

1 (25-ounce) jar tomato sauce or Buttery Tomato Sauce (page 93)

1¼ pounds mozzarella, shredded

● buttery tomato sauce

AN ELEGANT ITALIAN CLASSIC, this has to be the easiest tomato sauce to make. The butter adds a richness that elevates the sauce to great heights. It is best served at 7,500 feet over a mountain of pasta and topped with Parmesan.

1. Combine the tomatoes, onion, garlic, butter, and a large pinch of salt in a medium saucepan. Bring to a simmer over medium heat, lower the heat, and simmer uncovered, stirring occasionally, for 35 to 40 minutes, until the tomatoes are broken down and the sauce is thickened.

2. Discard the onion and taste for seasoning, adding salt and pepper as needed. Serve immediately, or let cool and then cover and refrigerate for up to 3 days or freeze for up to 1 month. Reheat in a saucepan over low heat, stirring frequently until heated through.

MAKES ABOUT 3 CUPS, OR ENOUGH FOR 1 POUND DRIED PASTA

1 (28-ounce) can whole peeled tomatoes, with juice, chopped

1 medium yellow onion, quartered

2 garlic cloves, minced

5 tablespoons unsalted butter

Salt and freshly ground black pepper

■ sauce bolognese

DUE TO POOR TIMING, a recent holiday weekend trip from New York to our ski destination in Vermont took an astonishing seven hours, including much-needed stops. We arrived at the house well past the dinner hour and hadn't shopped for groceries in recent memory. Luckily, there was a container of bolognese sauce in the freezer and a box of dry pasta on the counter. Twenty minutes later, we sat down to a comforting feast.

A classic bolognese sauce is simmered for hours to achieve its characteristic richness and soft texture. For this reason, it is perfectly suited to the slow cooker, although a bit of browning in a skillet beforehand helps build flavor. Although we usually favor quicker preparations than bolognese affords, the sauce has a great deal going for it: It is always popular, especially for milder palates (ahem, children), and it freezes well.

1. Heat the oil in a large skillet over high heat. When the oil is shimmering, add the cubed meat to the pan in one layer (you will most likely need to do this in batches) and brown it on all sides, about 6 minutes. Transfer the browned beef to a slow cooker insert. Repeat until all the cubes are browned.

2. Return the skillet to medium heat, add the carrots, and cook for 2 minutes. Add the onion and continue cooking until the vegetables are softened, about 4 minutes. Add the ground beef and cook, breaking the meat with a wooden spoon. When the meat is nearly cooked through (but not brown), about 5 minutes, add the garlic and continue cooking for 2 more minutes.

3. Add the wine and simmer until nearly all the liquid is evaporated, about 6 minutes. Add the milk and simmer until nearly all of the liquid evaporates, about 4 minutes.

SERVES 6 TO 8

3 tablespoons canola oil

1 pound chuck stew meat, cut into $3/_4$-inch pieces

2 small carrots, finely chopped

1 medium yellow onion, finely chopped

1 pound ground beef

2 garlic cloves, minced

1$1/_2$ cups dry white wine

1 cup whole milk

$1/_2$ teaspoon salt, plus more to taste

1 (28-ounce) can diced tomatoes

1 (28-ounce) can crushed or pureed tomatoes

Freshly ground black pepper

4. Transfer the ground beef mixture to the cooker and add the salt. Stir in the diced and crushed tomatoes. Cover the slow cooker and set it to low heat for 6 hours.

5. Stir the sauce, adjust the seasoning with salt and pepper, and serve immediately, or cool, cover, and freeze in small containers for up to 1 month. Reheat over medium-low heat until simmering, adding a little water if needed to prevent scorching.

fast food entrées

SOME PEOPLE WORK HARD AT SKIING FAST. They tune their equipment and point straight down the fall line. If they are smart, they also wear helmets.

We don't always have a need for speed on the slopes, but it's crucial in the kitchen if we want to maximize our time on the mountain. The "fast foods" in this chapter emphasize our favorite quick but polished preparations.

We aim for sophisticated results from the quickest-cooking cuts, such as pork chops, steaks, fish fillets, and chicken breasts. Burgers have always been fast, but our two zippy variations make them exciting again. Pan-roasting works well for these cuts, so we often finish them in the oven for even cooking. Quick pan sauces, using just a few ingredients, bring these recipes to a swift and tantalizing close. The two minutes we spend to create the sauce take the dish from good to fantastic and make cleaning the pan a breeze.

By finishing these dishes in the oven, we get less smoke in the room and less splatter. For the quickest cleanup, you can take the idea even further: For complete oven-baked simplicity with no browning, try Salmon Provençal with Stuffed Plum Tomatoes or Parmesan-Dijon Roasted Chicken Breasts.

For an elegant presentation, we offer two speedy roasts. The Roasted Beef Tenderloin with Red Wine–Shallot Reduction makes a straightforward but deeply satisfying meal, and the Roasted Pork Loin with Cherry Balsamic Pan Sauce is both succulent and affordable. The elongated shape of these cuts is critical to the speed at which they cook.

You'll be cooking so fast, you might want to wear your helmet in the kitchen.

how to defrost ground meat
in a microwave

WHOOPS, YOU FORGOT TO DEFROST the ground beef. Well, it is easy enough to use a microwave for this task—however, defrost meat this way only *immediately* before cooking it.

Remove the lump of ground meat from all packing material (including the paper and plastic or foam tray the meat is probably resting on). Place the meat in one piece on a plate; have a second plate handy as well. Using a 50 percent power setting, microwave the meat for 30 seconds. Remove the plate from the oven and feel the edges of the meat. If there are any soft (defrosted) sections, break them off, put them on the second plate, and set them aside. Flip the remaining frosty slab of meat and put it back in the microwave oven.

The goal is to remove defrosted meat from the microwave oven after it has defrosted but before it warms or cooks. A pile of cold-to-the-touch chunks of ground meat is the desired outcome.

Repeat the 30-second heating, breaking off the defrosted sections and setting them aside. If the meat is getting partially cooked during the 30-second intervals, switch to shorter intervals.

If you plan to brown and break up the meat as your next step, you can be a bit lazier and let the intervals go for a minute or so. Some of the meat may cook a bit more thoroughly than a perfect defrost, but you probably don't care much. If, on the other hand, you plan to mix the ground meat with seasonings or other ingredients, be vigilant about keeping the meat cold and uncooked.

If you do not have a microwave, you will have to use the warm water bath method to defrost (see page 110). Again, to be safe, perform this action *immediately* before you plan on cooking the meat.

● herbed turkey burgers

BURGERS ARE THE ULTIMATE FAST FOOD: They take mere minutes to prepare, minutes to cook, and minutes to eat. Fortunately, the ones you make yourself can actually be good for you, unlike the ones sold at fast food chains. Turkey burgers are a healthier option than ground beef patties, and adding fresh or dried herbs to the meat imparts tons of great flavor.

1. Combine the turkey, parsley, sage, thyme, mustard, salt, and pepper in a large bowl. Using your hands, lightly mix until just combined. Divide the meat evenly to form 4 patties, each about 3/4 inch thick.

2. Heat the oil in a large skillet or grill pan over medium-high heat. Add the turkey patties. Cook for 6 minutes, flip, and cook for 5 minutes more, or until browned and cooked through.

3. Serve immediately on toasted buns with the sliced avocado.

SERVES 4

1 1/2 pounds ground turkey

1 tablespoon chopped fresh parsley (optional)

1 tablespoon chopped fresh sage or 1 teaspoon dried

1 tablespoon chopped fresh thyme or 1 teaspoon dried

2 teaspoons Dijon mustard

1/2 teaspoon salt

1/4 teaspoon freshly ground black pepper

2 teaspoons vegetable oil

4 buns, split and toasted

1 avocado, sliced

■ blue cheese–stuffed bacon burgers

SOME WOULD ARGUE that a hamburger needs no improvement. But what can't be improved with bacon and its luscious partner, blue cheese? Though decadently flavored, this recipe takes just a few minutes longer to prepare than an ordinary, everyday burger. Cook up some bacon and then, while you're forming the patties, sneak a bit of blue cheese into the center of the meat. These will put to shame any burger sold in a ski lodge.

SERVES 4

6 slices thick-cut bacon

1¼ pounds ground sirloin

4 ounces blue cheese

Salt and freshly ground black pepper

4 buns, split and toasted

4 lettuce leaves

2 plum tomatoes, sliced

½ small red onion, sliced

1. Preheat the oven to 425°F.

2. Heat a large ovenproof skillet over medium heat. Add the bacon and cook until crisp, about 10 minutes. Remove the bacon to drain on paper towels. Pour off all but 2 tablespoons of the bacon fat from the skillet and set the skillet aside.

3. Put the ground sirloin in a medium bowl and crumble in the bacon slices. Gently mix the bacon with the meat. Form 4 equal patties, each about 1 inch thick.

4. Divide the cheese into 4 equal pieces. Using your thumb, make a well in the center of each burger and fill with a piece of cheese. Fold the meat over to fully enclose the cheese. Season all over with salt and pepper.

5. Return the skillet to medium-high heat. When the bacon fat is hot, add the burgers and cook for 3 minutes. Turn the burgers over and place the pan in the oven. Cook for 6 to 7 minutes for medium rare.

6. Serve on toasted buns with lettuce, tomato, and onion.

◆ roasted beef tenderloin with red wine–shallot reduction

THE LONG SHAPE OF THE TENDERLOIN means that it cooks remarkably quickly and evenly. If you monitor the cooking time and internal temperature, you will have a perfect piece of meat. While the roast rests, make a speedy reduction sauce with a bit of red wine for an elegant main course.

SERVES 4

1½ pounds beef tenderloin, trimmed

1 tablespoon extra-virgin olive oil

Salt and freshly ground black pepper

1 large shallot, thinly sliced

1 cup red wine

2 tablespoons unsalted butter

1. Remove the meat from the refrigerator 30 minutes before you plan on cooking it to let it come to room temperature.

2. Preheat the oven to 425°F.

3. Heat the oil in a large ovenproof skillet over medium-high heat. Season the beef generously on both sides with salt and pepper. When the pan is hot, add the meat and sear until browned on all sides, about 10 minutes total. Transfer the pan to the oven and roast for 20 to 25 minutes, or until a meat thermometer inserted into the center registers 135°F for medium rare.

4. Remove the beef from the pan and let rest for 10 minutes while you prepare the sauce.

5. Return the skillet to the stovetop over medium-high heat. Add the shallot and cook until softened, about 1 minute. Add the wine, stirring to loosen the browned bits from the bottom of the pan, and simmer until reduced to a glaze, about 6 minutes. Turn off the heat and stir in the butter until it is melted and the sauce is glossy.

6. To serve, slice the beef into ½-inch slices and top with the red wine sauce.

■ pan-roasted steaks in balsamic butter sauce

HAVE YOU EVER NOTICED that every ski town has a lousy steak joint? And that it's always crowded? Steak is one of the easiest foods to cook well at home; there is no need to stand in line for overpriced, inferior meat. And while the steaks rest, toss a few flavorful pantry ingredients into the pan and scrape it down to make an easy, delicious sauce. This deglazing process also makes cleanup a snap, since in making the sauce you loosen the tasty stuck-on browned bits from the pan. There will be no need to scrub.

SERVES 4

4 (8-ounce) filet mignon steaks or New York strip steaks

Salt and freshly ground black pepper

2 tablespoons vegetable oil

4 sprigs fresh rosemary (optional)

1 large shallot, minced, or 2 tablespoons minced onion

2 tablespoons balsamic vinegar

$\frac{1}{2}$ cup low-sodium beef or chicken broth

2 tablespoons unsalted butter

1. Take the meat out of the refrigerator 30 minutes before you plan on cooking it to let it come to room temperature.

2. Preheat the oven to 425°F.

3. Heat a large, heavy ovenproof skillet over high heat. Season the meat generously on both sides with salt and pepper. Add the oil to the pan and heat until shimmering. Add the steaks to the skillet and sear for 3 minutes, or until browned. Top each with a sprig of rosemary, if desired, flip, and then transfer the pan to the oven for 5 to 7 minutes for medium rare.

4. Transfer the steaks to a plate and let rest while you prepare the sauce. Return the skillet to medium-high heat. Add the shallot and cook for 2 minutes, stirring frequently. Add the vinegar and scrape the pan with a wooden spoon to loosen the browned bits. When the vinegar is evaporated, add the broth and allow the sauce to boil until it reduces to a glaze, about 4 minutes.

5. Turn off the heat and add the butter, stirring to combine. Spoon the sauce over the steaks and serve immediately.

parmesan-dijon roasted chicken breasts

HERE THREE MAIN FLAVORS—mustard, herbs, and Parmesan—combine to transform everyday chicken breasts into a meal so tasty and easy that we make it often.

1. Preheat the oven to 425°F.

2. In a small bowl, combine the mustard, oil, oregano, and parsley, if using. Season the chicken with salt and pepper and then brush all over with the mustard mixture.

3. Place the chicken breasts upside down on a rimmed baking sheet. Sprinkle evenly with half of the Parmesan. Turn the chicken over and coat with the remaining cheese, pressing lightly to adhere. Bake for 20 minutes, or until golden and cooked through.

4. Remove from the oven and let cool for 5 minutes before serving.

SERVES 4

1 tablespoon Dijon mustard

1 tablespoon extra-virgin olive oil

1 teaspoon chopped fresh oregano or $1/4$ teaspoon dried

$1/2$ teaspoon chopped fresh parsley (optional)

4 (6-ounce) boneless, skinless chicken breast halves

Salt and freshly ground black pepper

$2/3$ cup freshly grated Parmesan

■ chicken with tarragon cream sauce

WE'D LOVE TO SKI CHAMONIX in the French Alps, but—*quel dommage*—it hasn't happened yet. We'll have to settle for skiing stateside and making cream and tarragon sauce instead. This decadent-tasting dish is made entirely on the stovetop in a single pan and takes a lot less time (and money) than flying to France.

1. Heat the oil and butter in a large skillet over medium-high heat. Season the chicken all over with salt and pepper. Add the chicken to the pan and cook for 2 to 3 minutes on each side, or until browned but not cooked through. Transfer the chicken to a plate.

2. Reduce the heat to medium and add the shallot to the pan. Cook until softened, 1 to 2 minutes, stirring to loosen the browned bits from the bottom of the pan. Add the wine and cook until reduced to 1 tablespoon, about 4 minutes. Add the broth, cream, and 1 tablespoon of the tarragon. Return the chicken to the pan and simmer until cooked through, 6 to 7 minutes.

3. Transfer the chicken to a platter. Stir the remaining tarragon and lemon juice into the sauce. Taste and adjust the seasoning with salt and pepper. Pour the sauce over the chicken and serve immediately.

SERVES 4

1 tablespoon olive oil

1 tablespoon unsalted butter

4 (6-ounce) boneless, skinless chicken breast halves

Salt and freshly ground black pepper

1 large shallot, finely chopped, or 2 tablespoons chopped onion

¼ cup dry white wine

¼ cup low-sodium chicken broth

⅓ cup heavy cream

2 tablespoons chopped fresh tarragon or 2 teaspoons dried

1 teaspoon fresh lemon juice

■ feta-stuffed chicken breasts

WHILE BONELESS, SKINLESS CHICKEN breasts are the height of quick-cooking convenience, they often end up tough and dry. We avoid that problem here by stuffing them with a savory cheese mixture and drizzling a buttery pan sauce on top.

SERVES 4

4 ounces feta

4 garlic cloves, minced

Grated zest of $1/2$ lemon

4 tablespoons extra-virgin olive oil

4 (6-ounce) boneless, skinless chicken breast halves

4 small sprigs fresh oregano or 1 teaspoon dried

Salt and freshly ground black pepper

1 tablespoon plus 1 teaspoon white balsamic vinegar

$1/3$ cup low-sodium chicken broth

$1^1/2$ tablespoons unsalted butter

1. Preheat the oven to 400°F.

2. In a small bowl, crumble the cheese with a fork. Add the garlic, lemon zest, and 2 tablespoons of the oil and stir to combine.

3. Using a sharp paring knife, make a 2- to 3-inch slit horizontally in the thicker side of each chicken breast. Do not cut all the way through. Push one-quarter of the cheese mixture into each slit, add a sprig of oregano, and close as well as possible.

4. Heat the remaining 2 tablespoons oil in a large skillet over medium-high heat. Season the chicken all over with salt and pepper. When the oil is hot and nearly smoking, carefully place the breasts upside down in the pan and cook for 4 minutes, or until browned. Carefully flip the breasts, using a spatula in one hand and a fork in the other, and transfer the pan to the oven. Bake for 25 minutes, or until the center of the breast registers 165°F on an instant-read thermometer.

5. Remove the chicken from the pan and set aside on a platter to rest while you prepare the sauce. Place the pan over medium-high heat and add the vinegar. Cook for 1 minute, scraping the pan bottom with a spatula to combine any browned chicken or bits of cheese with the sauce. Add the broth and reduce the liquid by half, about 5 minutes. Turn off the heat and stir in the butter to melt.

6. Place each breast on a plate, drizzle the sauce over each, and serve immediately.

■ pan-roasted chicken breasts

PAN-ROASTING WHOLE bone-in chicken breasts is our shortcut way of getting great flavor without roasting a whole chicken. We start the highly seasoned chicken in a hot pan to get the cooking process going with direct heat and then finish the chicken in the oven to cook it evenly and to keep kitchen smokiness at bay. This gives us several great results: juicy meat, crisp skin, and a flavorful pan sauce.

1. Preheat the oven to 400°F.

2. Loosen the skin from the chicken breasts. Combine the rosemary, lemon zest, and garlic and rub the mixture under the skin. Season the breasts all over with salt and pepper.

3. Place a large ovenproof skillet over medium-high heat and add the oil and butter. When hot, place the chicken, breast side down, in the pan. Cook without moving for 5 minutes. Turn the chicken over and place the pan in the oven. Bake for 25 to 30 minutes, or until the chicken is cooked through.

4. Transfer the chicken to a platter to rest while you prepare the sauce. Place the hot pan on the stovetop over medium heat. Add the shallot and cook for 1 minute. Add the wine and cook for 2 minutes, scraping up the browned bits from the bottom of the pan. Add the broth and any accumulated juices from the platter where the chicken is resting and cook for 5 minutes, or until the sauce is reduced slightly. Turn off the heat and stir in the butter until thoroughly incorporated. Stir in the parsley, if desired.

5. Cut the chicken breasts in half and pour the pan sauce over them before serving.

SERVES 4

Chicken

2 whole bone-in chicken breasts (about 4 pounds)

1 tablespoon chopped fresh rosemary or 1 teaspoon dried

1 teaspoon grated lemon zest

1 garlic clove, minced

Salt and freshly ground black pepper

1 tablespoon olive oil

1 tablespoon unsalted butter

Sauce

1 medium shallot, minced, or 2 tablespoons minced onion

1/3 cup dry white wine

2/3 cup low-sodium chicken broth

2 tablespoons unsalted butter, cold

1 tablespoon chopped fresh parsley (optional)

roasted pork loin with cherry balsamic pan sauce

THIS IS A SURPRISINGLY FAST way to put a roast on the table. The sauce is done while the roast rests, so you can use the half hour or so cooking time to make a side dish, set the table, change out of your ski gear, or sit back with a cocktail— or perhaps all of these, if you're especially quick on your feet.

1. Preheat the oven to 400°F.

2. Heat the oil in a large ovenproof skillet or roasting pan over high heat. Generously salt and pepper the roast. When the pan is hot, add the roast and brown on all sides, 2 to 3 minutes per side.

3. Transfer the pan to the oven. Roast the pork until an instant-read thermometer reads 140°F when inserted into the thickest part of the roast, 20 to 30 minutes.

4. Remove the roast to a platter and let rest for 5 minutes while you prepare the sauce. While it rests, the temperature of the roast should rise to 145° or 150°F. Return the pan to medium-high heat and add the shallot. Cook for 2 minutes, add the vinegar, and scrape the pan with a wooden spoon. When the vinegar is reduced to a glaze, about 5 minutes, add the broth and reduce again by half, about 7 minutes. Add the cherries and syrup and simmer for 3 minutes. Remove from the heat.

5. Slice the roast thinly, drizzle the sauce over the meat, and serve immediately.

SERVES 4 TO 6

2 tablespoons vegetable oil

Salt and freshly ground black pepper

2½- to 3-pound pork loin roast, tied

1 large shallot, minced, or 2 tablespoons minced onion

⅓ cup balsamic vinegar

½ cup low-sodium chicken broth

¾ cup jarred pitted sour cherries, sliced in half, plus 2 tablespoons reserved syrup from the jar

defrosting steaks, chops, or chicken pieces

THE SAFEST AND EASIEST WAY to defrost meat is overnight in the refrigerator. Sometimes we forget, however, or find that the refrigerator is so cold that the meat is still partially frozen the next day. Don't call the local pizzeria just yet, though. You can defrost food quickly and safely, provided you will be cooking it immediately.

Fill the sink with lukewarm water. If you are lucky enough to have purchased vacuum-packed meat, simply drop it into the bath. If you have a standard pack, wrapped with either paper or foam and plastic, you'll need to unwrap the meat (discard any foam trays) and put it in sealable plastic bags. Seal the bags carefully, pressing out all air, and slip them into the water bath. The more separate the pieces of meat are from one another—that is, the more bags you use—the quicker and gentler the defrosting process will be.

After a few minutes, the water bath will become cold. Drain the water from the sink and refill it with lukewarm water.

Two to three baths should do the trick. Lightly squeeze the meat in the middle as well as at the edges to confirm a successful defrosting. If any water has leaked into the zipper bags, pat the meat dry with paper towels before seasoning.

Cook the meat *immediately* after defrosting.

● pan-roasted pork chops with herbed butter

ONE EXCELLENT WAY to produce a flavorful main course quickly is to garnish meat or fish with a pat of compound butter. It melts into a silky sauce as you carry the plates from the kitchen into the dining room. Here, pork chops get this swift, effective treatment. You can even make the herbed butter well in advance and freeze or refrigerate it. Serve this dish with an equally speedy side dish, such as Couscous with Currants (page 148) or a roasted vegetable.

1. In a small bowl, combine the butter, shallots, parsley (if using), and rosemary. Mash with a fork until well blended. Turn the butter mixture onto a sheet of wax paper and form into a log. Refrigerate or wrap in a freezer bag and freeze for up to 1 month.

2. Preheat the oven to 425°F.

3. In an ovenproof skillet large enough to hold the chops in a single layer, heat the oil over high heat until it shimmers. Season the chops generously with salt and pepper and add to the pan. Cook until browned on one side, about 3 minutes, then flip them over and transfer the pan to the oven. Bake until cooked through but still moist and juicy, about 7 minutes.

4. Cut the butter log into 4 pieces. Remove the chops from the oven and transfer to plates or a serving platter. Top each chop with a pat of herbed butter and serve immediately.

SERVES 4

6 tablespoons unsalted butter, slightly softened and cut into 1/2-inch pieces

2 teaspoons minced shallots

2 teaspoons minced fresh parsley (optional)

1/2 teaspoon minced fresh rosemary or a pinch of dried

2 tablespoons canola or other vegetable oil

4 thin-cut, bone-in pork chops (about 2 pounds)

Salt and freshly ground black pepper

• chili-spiced salmon

THERE'S MORE THAN ONE WAY to get your chili fix. Here we use typical chili spices to make a tasty dry rub for salmon fillets. If chili is a favorite in your home, you'll already have all of the spices on hand.

---

1. Preheat the oven to 425°F.

2. Combine the chili powder, cumin, oregano, salt, pepper, and cayenne in a shallow dish. Coat the salmon fillets with the spice mixture.

3. Place a large ovenproof skillet, preferrably nonstick, over medium-high heat. When the skillet is hot, add the oil and swirl to coat the bottom. Place the seasoned salmon, skin side down, in the skillet. Once the salmon is browned, about 3 minutes, flip the fillets and transfer the pan to the oven to roast for an additional 7 to 9 minutes, depending on the thickness of the fillets and your preference. We like our salmon cooked to medium, when it is still a little pink in the center.

4. Transfer to plates and serve with lemon wedges for squeezing on top.

SERVES 4

3 tablespoons chili powder

1 teaspoon ground cumin

1 teaspoon dried oregano

$3/4$ teaspoon kosher salt

$1/4$ teaspoon freshly ground black pepper

$1/4$ teaspoon cayenne

4 (6-ounce) salmon fillets, skin on

2 teaspoons vegetable oil

1 lemon, cut into wedges

salmon provençal with stuffed plum tomatoes

WE MOSTLY AVOID the grocery store's selection of so-called fresh tomatoes in winter, when they are mealy and flavorless. However, meaty plum tomatoes are a decent option because they have good texture and flavor when cooked. This dish saves time by cooking a hot side dish along with the main event. If only we could figure out how to wait in the lift line just once for two runs . . .

SERVES 4

6 large plum tomatoes

1 garlic clove, minced

1 large shallot, minced

1 tablespoon capers, packed in vinegar, drained

$1/2$ cup chopped kalamata or other flavorful black olives

2 tablespoons chopped fresh parsley (optional)

$1/2$ teaspoon dried thyme

$3/4$ cup panko bread crumbs or plain dried bread crumbs

$1/4$ cup plus 2 tablespoons olive oil

4 (8-ounce) salmon fillets, skin on

1. Preheat the oven to 400°F.

2. Dice 2 of the tomatoes finely and set aside. Slice the other 4 in half lengthwise and scrape out the seeds with your fingers, leaving the ribs intact.

3. Combine the garlic, shallot, capers, olives, parsley, if using, thyme, bread crumbs, and $1/4$ cup of the oil in a small bowl. Set aside.

4. Brush the salmon fillets on all sides with the remaining 2 tablespoons oil. Set the fillets, skin side down, in one layer in a large baking dish. Place the tomato halves, cut sides up, around the fish. Carefully mound 2 teaspoons of the olive mixture into each tomato half.

5. Add the diced tomatoes to the remaining olive mixture and stir to combine. Mound 1 heaping tablespoon of the mixture carefully onto each salmon fillet.

6. Bake the fish and tomatoes for about 15 minutes, or until the fish is nearly cooked through and the tomatoes are soft. Serve immediately.

• jibbers' enchiladas

TO JIB IS TO HUCK ONESELF off a terrain park feature, then to twist or grab or otherwise impress the public before landing, upright of course, and skiing on down the hill. If you do that a few times in a day, you'll need a hearty portion of these enchiladas, along with a great big margarita. (Depending on the angle of your landings, maybe aspirin as well.) Because this dish utilizes leftover chicken (or beef or pork), it is the perfectly simple end to a hectic day. Assemble the enchiladas from ingredients you already have on hand and serve last night's meal once again, but in a zesty disguise.

SERVES 3 TO 4

3 cups (12 ounces) shredded Monterey Jack or mild Cheddar

10 (6-inch) corn or flour tortillas

1 (19-ounce) can enchilada sauce

2 cups cubed or shredded cooked chicken, beef, pork, or turkey

1 large sweet onion, finely diced

1. Preheat the oven to 375°F.

2. Grease the bottom of a 9 x 13-inch baking dish. Set aside 1 cup of the cheese to sprinkle on top.

3. Coat one side of each tortilla with enchilada sauce. Drop a small portion of the chicken, onion, and cheese on each tortilla. Roll the tortillas into tubes around the filling and place in the prepared pan. Pack the enchiladas tightly in one layer. Pour the remaining sauce over the dish and sprinkle the reserved cheese on top.

4. Wrap the dish tightly with foil and bake for 35 minutes, or until the sauce sizzles. Remove the foil and bake for another 15 minutes, or until the cheese is browning on top.

5. Transfer the enchiladas to plates and spoon any sauce from the bottom of the baking dish on top.

NOTE After step 3, the dish can be tightly wrapped and frozen for up to 1 month. Bake, covered, for 50 minutes at 375°F until the sauce sizzles, and then uncovered for an additional 15 minutes.

slow food entrées

THE APPEAL OF SLOW-COOKED FOOD is twofold. Long-braised meats are fork-tender comfort dishes that fill the house with warm, magnificent smells. More practically, slow cooking also offers come-in-and-sit-right-down convenience, since all the preparation is done ahead of time.

We offer several recipes with multiple unattended hours of cooking time. A slow cooker, or crock-pot, is a great tool for cooking this way. While many voices exuberantly proclaim that anything can be made in a slow cooker, we've chosen our recipes carefully. Not every cut of meat benefits from six hours left to its own devices. Large cuts such as pork shoulder and brisket do, however. Because our slow-cooker recipes are meant to be the height of convenience, we mostly avoid first browning meats in a separate pan on the stove. We don't want to stand in the kitchen scrubbing a skillet while everyone else is zipping up their jackets and hitting the slopes.

For a few recipes, however, browning is an absolute must. Chili requires this extra step, and it also benefits from using two forms of beef, ground and cubed.

When browning is required, as for beef stew, we have a trick to share: You can use the oven itself as the slow cooker by browning the meat in a Dutch oven and then setting it in a low-temperature oven for several hours. Since the meat browns and stews in the same vessel, you have only one pot to clean at the end of the cooking process.

Needless to say, all of these dishes can be prepared a day or two in advance and refrigerated or even frozen for up to a month.

■ chunky beef stew

THIS RECIPE USES THE OVEN as the slow cooker. Browning the meat is a must for building flavor in a stew, but we decided we'd rather not clean two pans—one for browning and then the slow cooker. Instead, this dish cooks in the same pot you use for browning. Most beef stew recipes also require adding vegetables in a certain sequence at the end of the cooking time, so they don't turn to mush. We've solved that problem by following a hint from a recipe that appeared in *Cooks Country* magazine: Our vegetables dry-roast in the oven alongside the simmering stew. After many hours in the oven, they are still toothsome.

1. Adjust the oven racks to accommodate a Dutch oven or large covered pot. Preheat the oven to 250°F.

2. Heat the vegetable oil in a large Dutch oven over medium-high heat. Generously salt and pepper the beef. Brown the meat, in stages, so as not to crowd the pan. Each batch should take about 10 minutes.

3. Remove the browned beef to a plate and add the onions to the pot. Cook for 5 minutes, or until the onions begin to brown. Add the garlic and cook until fragrant, 1 to 2 minutes. Add the tomato paste, flour, and soy sauce and cook for 1 to 2 minutes. Add the broth and scrape any browned meat bits off the bottom and sides of the pan.

4. Return the beef to the pot, add the bay leaves, and bring to a boil. Cover the pot and place in the oven. Set the oven timer for 6 hours.

5. Chop the potatoes and carrots into 1 1/2-inch cubes. Pile the vegetables into the smallest covered baking dish that will accommodate them. Drizzle the olive oil over the vegetables, sprinkle the thyme and rosemary on top, and stir to coat. Cover and place in the oven.

6. After 6 hours, remove the meat and vegetables from the oven. Stir the peas into the stew. Divide the vegetables among 4 shallow bowls. Discard the bay leaves. Ladle the beef stew over the vegetables and serve hot.

SERVES 4

3 tablespoons vegetable oil, or cooking spray, as needed

Salt and freshly ground black pepper

4 to 5 pounds beef chuck, trimmed of excess fat and cut into 1 1/2-inch cubes

2 medium yellow onions, cut into 1-inch dice

4 garlic cloves, coarsely chopped

1 (6-ounce) can tomato paste

2 tablespoons all-purpose flour

2 tablespoons soy sauce

1 (16-ounce) can low-sodium chicken broth

2 bay leaves

6 large red potatoes (about 2 pounds)

3 to 4 large carrots (about 1 1/2 pounds)

2 tablespoons olive oil

1 teaspoon dried thyme

1/2 teaspoon dried rosemary

1 cup frozen peas, thawed

getting the most out of your slow cooker

USING A SLOW COOKER IS SIMPLE: You plug it in, put the top on, and turn it on to low or high. The cooker slowly comes to a low, even cooking temperature.

When you add your meat, often unbrowned, to the pot with a few vegetables and some liquid, you may experience a moment of doubt when you turn the switch. Nothing seems to happen. This is quite different than the reassuring sizzle of meat placed in a hot skillet on the stove. Over the first two hours of cooking time, the slow cooker comes to temperature and steam forms on the inner surface of the lid.

After about two hours, some foods have an unappealing gray color, but don't worry! The meat will slowly continue to cook, rendering its fat into a liquid, softening and browning the meat to yield a fork-tender texture that is the signature of braising. While many slow-cooker recipes are written for eight-hour cook times, we feel most foods taste better at four to six hours of cook time. When the meat is no longer gray and is tender enough to break apart when pushed with a fork, it is done.

Many slow cookers have a warm setting that automatically kicks in when the pre-set cook time ends. In our tests, the interior temperature of the pot did not fall very quickly on the warm setting. If a recipe specifies, say, a six-hour cooking time, and you think you might not make it home right away, try a four-hour cook time and maybe three hours on warm. This should avoid overcooking the food, unlike a six-hour cook time plus one hour at warm.

● brisket with sweet mustard sauce

BRISKET IS OUR FAVORITE CUT OF BEEF for pot-roasting. This preparation, with its slightly sweetened mustard sauce, goes over well with the whole crowd. The meat need not be browned before braising in a slow cooker. The brown sugar caramelizes, so the brisket develops a rich brown color as it cooks.

---

1. The night before serving the brisket, combine the mustard, sugar, garlic, salt, and pepper in a blender or food processor and process until smooth. Alternatively, mince the garlic finely by hand and whisk the ingredients together.

2. Peel the onions and cut each into 8 wedges. Scatter them over the bottom of the slow cooker insert. Rub the mustard mixture all over the beef and set over the onions. Cover the pot and refrigerate overnight or for at least 2 hours.

3. Remove the pot from the refrigerator, pour in the broth, and slow-cook on the low setting for 7 to 7$\frac{1}{2}$ hours.

4. Transfer the meat from the pot to a cutting board. Remove the onions and 1 to 2 cups cooking liquid to a blender. Puree with $\frac{1}{2}$ teaspoon cornstarch per cup of cooking liquid. Slice the brisket thinly against the grain and transfer to a platter. Drizzle the sauce over the meat and serve in sandwich rolls or with potatoes.

SERVES 6 TO 8

$\frac{1}{3}$ cup Dijon mustard

$\frac{1}{3}$ cup brown sugar

5 garlic cloves

$\frac{1}{2}$ teaspoon salt

Pinch of freshly ground black pepper

2 medium yellow onions

4 to 5 pounds brisket in 2 or 3 pieces, trimmed of excess fat

1 cup low-sodium beef or chicken broth

$\frac{1}{2}$ to 1 teaspoon cornstarch

mogul beef chili

THIS IS A CLASSIC RED CHILI dressed up with fork-tender chunks of beef and a rich gravy. The recipe proves that the slow cooker is not merely a tool of convenience but actually a superior way to cook certain foods. Although you'll need to brown the meat before you put it into the slow cooker, the results are well worth the effort—and the house will smell amazing when you come home.

SERVES 4

3 tablespoons vegetable oil

2 medium yellow onions, chopped

1 red or green bell pepper, cut into ½-inch pieces

5 garlic cloves, chopped

¼ cup chili powder

1 tablespoon ground cumin

2 teaspoons ground coriander

1 teaspoon dried oregano

1 teaspoon cayenne

¼ teaspoon red pepper flakes

12 ounces ground beef

Salt and freshly ground black pepper

1½ pounds chuck stew meat, cut into 1-inch cubes

1 (28-ounce) can diced tomatoes

1 (28-ounce) can crushed or pureed tomatoes

2 (14-ounce) cans red kidney beans, drained and rinsed

1. Heat 2 tablespoons of the oil in a large, heavy skillet or Dutch oven over medium heat. Add the onions, bell pepper, garlic, chili powder, cumin, coriander, oregano, cayenne, and red pepper flakes. Cook until the vegetables have softened, about 6 minutes. Scrape the vegetables into the slow cooker insert.

2. Return the skillet to medium-high heat and add the beef. Season with salt and pepper and cook, breaking up the beef with a spoon until browned, about 6 minutes. Transfer to the slow cooker.

3. Return the skillet to medium-high heat and add the remaining tablespoon oil. Salt and pepper the cubed beef on all sides. When the skillet is hot and the oil is just beginning to smoke, add the cubed beef in one layer. Brown the cubes well on all sides, 5 to 7 minutes, and then transfer to the slow cooker.

4. Return the skillet to medium-high heat and add ¼ cup water. Scrape the skillet with a wooden spoon as the water boils, loosening all of the cooked bits from the bottom. Pour the liquid into the slow cooker.

5. Add the diced and crushed tomatoes and the beans, stir everything together, cover, and cook on high for 6 hours, or until the beef cubes are fork tender.

6. Remove the largest chunks of beef one at a time to a plate. Using two forks, shred the meat, and then replace it in the pot. (This step is optional, but it makes for the best chili texture.) Stir the chili and serve hot.

■ white chicken chili

LET NO ONE SUGGEST that we don't embrace snowboarding. We embrace it as an alternative to the more traditional way of getting down the mountain. In much the same way, our White Chicken Chili offers an alternative to the traditional beefy red version. It's just as hearty and satisfying as a red chili, and the flavors are just a little brighter. Eat up, and you'll be ready to go back out and face whatever the mountain has in store for you.

1. Cover the beans with cool water and soak overnight. Alternatively, place the beans in a medium saucepan, cover with water, and bring to a boil. Cover and let sit off the heat for 1 hour.

2. Heat the oil in a large pot over medium heat. Add the garlic, onion, and chiles and cook until softened, about 5 minutes. Add the cumin, oregano, cayenne, salt, pepper, and red pepper flakes and cook for 1 minute more. Stir in the broth and bring to a boil. Drain the beans and add to the pot. Lower the heat so the broth simmers and add the chicken. Cook until the chicken is cooked through, about 20 minutes.

3. Remove the chicken from the pot and transfer to a cutting board. Using two forks, shred the chicken, and then return it to the pot. Continue to simmer, stirring occasionally, for about 45 minutes, until the beans are tender.

4. Taste and adjust the seasoning. Serve with cilantro, cheese, and lime wedges for squeezing on top.

SERVES 4 TO 6

1 pound dried white beans, such as cannellini or Great Northern, rinsed and picked over

1 tablespoon extra-virgin olive oil

5 garlic cloves, minced

1 large yellow onion, diced

2 (4$^{1}/_{2}$-ounce) cans chopped green chiles

1 tablespoon ground cumin

1 tablespoon dried oregano

$^{1}/_{2}$ teaspoon cayenne

$^{1}/_{2}$ teaspoon salt

$^{1}/_{4}$ teaspoon freshly ground black pepper

$^{1}/_{4}$ teaspoon red pepper flakes

5 cups low-sodium chicken broth

1 pound boneless, skinless chicken breast halves

Chopped fresh cilantro

Shredded Monterey Jack

Lime wedges

● beef short ribs, asian style

SHORT RIBS ARE A WONDERFULLY FATTY cut of meat for braising. We make enough for a small crowd here by cooking a substantial amount. This allows us to get a cooking time of 5½ to 6 hours in the slow cooker. If you cook less meat, the dish will be done faster. Serve this over bowls of steamed rice or noodles and topped with chopped scallions.

---

1. Whisk the shallots, soy sauce, sugar, broth, and sesame oil together in a small bowl.

2. Generously season the ribs with pepper. Place 1 rib in the slow cooker insert and pour some of the sauce mixture over it. Put 2 slices of the ginger on the meat. Layer more ribs, sauce, and ginger into the cooker. Pour any remaining sauce on top. Scatter the star anise in the cooker. Break the cinnamon stick into 2 pieces and add to the cooker.

3. Cover and cook on high for 6 hours, or until the meat is tender enough to break apart with a fork.

4. Transfer the meat to a platter. Remove 2 cups of the cooking liquid into a clear measuring cup or fat separator. Because short ribs are such a fatty cut, extra fat will rise to the surface. Pour or spoon off this fat and then pour the remaining juices over the meat. Serve hot.

SERVES 6 TO 8

2 shallots or ½ small yellow onion, finely chopped

½ cup soy sauce

¼ cup brown sugar

¼ cup low-sodium beef or chicken broth or water

2 tablespoons dark sesame oil

5 to 6 pounds boneless beef short ribs

Freshly ground black pepper

8 thin slices fresh ginger

4 whole star anise

1 (3-inch) cinnamon stick

● spicy pulled pork

THIS IS THE QUINTESSENTIAL SLOW-COOKER RECIPE: It requires no browning and can stand up to six hours of cooking time without becoming overdone. You can ski from first tracks until the lifts close, and then stagger in and sit down to a hot meal. Serve this peppery meat cut into chunks with rice and vegetables. Alternatively, tease it into shreds with two forks and serve on sandwich rolls with your favorite barbecue sauce.

1. The night before cooking, stir together the paprika, chili powder, cumin, salt, pepper, cayenne, oregano, cinnamon, and sugar in a small bowl.

2. Trim the pork shoulder of excess fat and the thick layer of skin that often comes attached to one side of the meat. Cut the roast into 2 large pieces. Try to make the cut in a way that creates a lot of surface area. In other words, if the meat has an oblong shape, cut it lengthwise to make 2 thinner oblong pieces.

3. Rub the spices all over the meat. Wrap the meat in plastic wrap or place it in a covered baking dish and refrigerate overnight.

4. In the morning, cut the onions into 2-inch chunks and scatter them on the bottom of the slow cooker insert. Unwrap the meat and place one piece on top of the onions. Pour half of the can of tomatoes over the meat, then place the other piece in the pot and repeat. The liquid in the pot may not cover the meat, which is fine.

5. Turn on the slow cooker to the high setting for 6 hours. Most slow cookers switch to a warming setting after their cook time. This dish can remain at that setting for an additional hour without becoming overcooked.

6. Using tongs or a slotted spoon, carefully transfer the meat to a serving platter. It should be falling apart.

7. Use a slotted spoon to distribute the vegetables over the steaming meat. Drizzle some of the cooking liquid over the food and serve immediately.

SERVES 4 TO 6

1/4 cup paprika

2 tablespoons chili powder

2 tablespoons ground cumin

2 tablespoons salt

2 tablespoons freshly ground black pepper

1 teaspoon cayenne

1 tablespoon dried oregano

1 teaspoon ground cinnamon

3 tablespoons light brown sugar

5 to 6 pounds boneless pork shoulder

2 medium yellow onions

1 (28-ounce) can diced tomatoes

● cider-maple pork shoulder

PORK SHOULDER, also called picnic roast, is perfect for braising. This big cut of meat loves the slow treatment—hours and hours at a low temperature. The abundant fat in the meat renders over time and keeps everything moist until dinnertime. The resulting consistency means you can leave the knives in the drawer.

---

1. The night before cooking, trim the pork shoulder of excess fat and trim off the thick layer of skin that often comes attached to one side of the meat. Cut the roast into 2 large pieces.

2. Stir the sugar, cinnamon, ginger, and allspice together in a small bowl. Rub the spices generously all over the meat. Wrap the meat in plastic wrap or place it in a covered baking dish. Refrigerate the meat overnight.

3. In the morning, peel and cut the onions into 2-inch chunks and place them at the bottom of the slow cooker insert. Stir in the cider and soy sauce. Place the meat pieces on top. Turn on the slow cooker to high for 6 hours. Many slow cookers switch to a warming setting after their cook time. This dish can remain at that setting for an additional hour without becoming overcooked.

4. Using tongs or a slotted spoon, transfer the meat to a serving platter. Strain the cooking juices into a bowl. If a lot of fat rises to the surface, spoon it off and discard. For each ¹/₂ cup liquid, whisk in 2 tablespoons maple syrup. Drizzle the sauce over the resting meat and serve.

SERVES 6

5 to 6 pounds boneless pork shoulder

¹/₂ cup brown sugar

2 tablespoons ground cinnamon

4 teaspoons ground ginger

1 teaspoon ground allspice

2 medium yellow onions

1¹/₂ cups apple cider

¹/₄ cup soy sauce

2 to 4 tablespoons maple syrup

◆ coq au vin

A CLASSIC FRENCH STEW, coq au vin is simply chicken simmered in red wine. We find that roasting the mushrooms separately intensifies their flavor. This trick makes supper just a bit more elegant—like jumping the cornice lip instead of merely pointing downhill.

---

1. Preheat the oven to 425°F. Toss the mushrooms with the oil, season with salt and pepper, and place on a rimmed baking sheet. Roast for 20 to 25 minutes, or until well browned. Remove from the oven and set aside.

2. Heat a large, wide, heavy pot over medium heat. Add the bacon and cook until crisp, about 8 minutes. Remove the bacon to drain on paper towels. Reserve the bacon fat in the pot.

3. Turn the heat under the pot to medium-high. Pat the chicken pieces dry and season with salt and pepper. Cook in batches in the bacon fat until golden brown, about 5 minutes per side. Transfer to a platter and set aside.

4. Discard all but 2 tablespoons of fat from the pot and reduce the heat to medium. Add the onion and garlic and cook until translucent, about 6 minutes. Add the thyme, bay leaf, tomato paste, and red wine and bring to a boil, scraping the bottom of the pan to release any browned bits. Add the chicken, cover the pan, and reduce the heat to medium-low. Simmer for 30 minutes. Add the roasted mushrooms and cook for 30 minutes longer.

5. Transfer the chicken to a platter. Combine the butter and flour in a small bowl to form a smooth paste. Whisk the paste into the cooking liquid and increase the heat to bring to a boil. Cook until the sauce is thickened and reduced, about 8 minutes.

6. Remove the bay leaf and thyme sprigs and discard. Crumble in the bacon and return the chicken to the pot. Remove from the heat, sprinkle with parsley, if desired, and serve immediately.

SERVES 4 TO 6

1¼ pounds white button or cremini mushrooms, trimmed and cut in half if large

1 tablespoon olive oil

Salt and freshly ground black pepper

4 slices thick-cut bacon

8 pieces chicken, about 4 pounds (2 breasts, 2 wings, 2 thighs, 2 drumsticks)

1 large yellow onion, halved and thinly sliced

3 garlic cloves, minced

4 sprigs fresh thyme or 2 teaspoons dried

1 bay leaf

1 tablespoon tomato paste

1 (750-ml) bottle red wine

2 tablespoons unsalted butter, room temperature

2 tablespoons all-purpose flour

¼ cup chopped fresh parsley (optional)

salads and sides

WHEN WE'VE OUTDONE OURSELVES with a weekend menu of hot and hearty dishes, we yearn for a crisp salad. Although salad creation is effortless in the summertime, with its abundance of seasonal vegetables, there is no reason why a wintertime salad should disappoint. To fight the cold-weather salad blues, choose ingredients carefully. Skip right past the tomatoes—which are dreary and tasteless in January—in favor of apples, beets, and nuts. And in the "if you can't beat 'em, join 'em" category, try an iceberg lettuce wedge with blue cheese as a throwback to your youth.

We also make our own salad dressings, since they taste so much better than anything you can find in a bottle. Two basic vinaigrettes can see you through any salad situation. Traditional Dijon balsamic dressing is thick and zesty. A lighter, fruitier white balsamic shallot vinaigrette goes well with fruits and other acidic ingredients.

Beyond salads, we love to see fresh seasonal vegetables on our plate. The most popular offering in this chapter is Roasted Brussels Sprouts with Bacon. Guests have to be physically restrained from eating it before the meal is served. It smells that good. And don't overlook the excellent quality of many frozen vegetables these days. Frozen peas are a particular favorite, not only for their convenience but also for their superb taste. We add them to soups and pastas and even turn them into their own delicious side dish.

Finally, what would comforting winter food be without potatoes, roasted, smashed with roasted garlic, or blanketed in a cheese gratin? Alternatively, we serve up sweet potato fries and a blazing fast couscous dish with currants and scallions.

■ beet, endive, and roquefort salad

THIS CLASSIC SALAD is the perfect vehicle for wintertime ingredients. We think beets are delicious roasted, and their sweetness intensifies when they are paired with a piquant Roquefort—it's an unbeatable combination.

---

1. Preheat the oven to 400°F.

2. Wrap the beets individually in heavy-duty aluminum foil and place on a baking sheet. Bake for 45 minutes to 1 hour, depending on the size of the beets, until easily pierced with a knife. Open the foil packages and let the beets cool thoroughly.

3. While the beets are cooling, toast the walnut halves on a baking sheet in the oven, shaking the pan occasionally, until fragrant and lightly browned, about 10 minutes. Set aside to cool.

4. Slice the endives in half lengthwise. Remove the bottom cores and cut the endives crosswise into 1-inch pieces. Put the endive pieces in a large mixing bowl and add the walnuts, cheese, and pear. Season with about half the vinaigrette.

5. Using paper towels, remove the skins of the beets and then dice them. Place the beets in a medium bowl with the remaining vinaigrette and a pinch of salt and pepper. Toss to coat.

6. Add the beets to the endive mixture and carefully stir just to combine. Serve immediately, topped with pepper.

SERVES 6

6 medium beets (about 1³/₄ pounds), tops trimmed

1 cup walnut halves or pieces

3 Belgian endives

2¹/₂ ounces Roquefort, crumbled (about ²/₃ cup)

1 pear, ripe but firm, thinly sliced

About ¹/₂ cup Dijon-Balsamic Vinaigrette (recipe follows)

Salt and freshly ground black pepper

dijon-balsamic vinaigrette

Our friend Adrienne makes vinaigrettes that are always perfectly balanced and tasty. She learned to make them while living in France, where she also skis. We like Adrienne in spite of her glamorous lifestyle, especially since she shared her foolproof recipe with us. This vinaigrette is great for robust or composed salads and bitter greens.

MAKES ABOUT 1 CUP

1 garlic clove, cut in half

1 tablespoon plus 1 teaspoon Dijon mustard

3 tablespoons balsamic vinegar

3/4 cup extra-virgin olive oil

Salt and freshly ground black pepper

1. Rub the garlic clove all over the inside of a small bowl. Reserve the garlic.

2. Add the mustard and vinegar to the bowl and whisk to combine. Slowly drizzle in the oil, whisking constantly until the vinaigrette is emulsified. Alternatively, you can use a blender. Add salt and pepper to taste.

3. Add the garlic clove halves to the vinaigrette for a more intense garlic flavor. Remove before serving. The vinaigrette will keep in an airtight container in the refrigerator for up to 5 days.

● winter romaine salad

THERE'S NO POINT in buying most grocery store tomatoes in winter. Instead, we use fruit to perk up our cold-weather salads. This version, featuring tart apples, makes a crisp counterpoint to savory main dishes.

1. Toss the lettuce and apple slices together in a serving bowl. Add the vinaigrette and toss to combine. Top with the almonds.

2. Using a vegetable peeler, make thin curls from the block of cheese and add to the top of the salad. Serve immediately.

SERVES 4

2 hearts of romaine lettuce, torn into bite-size pieces

1 Granny Smith apple, thinly sliced

White Balsamic Shallot Vinaigrette (recipe follows)

$1/2$ cup roasted unsalted almonds, whole or slivered

2-ounce block Parmesan

white balsamic shallot vinaigrette

This lovely fruity vinaigrette is the house dressing in Sarah's kitchen. It pairs beautifully with salads that have fruit in them. White balsamic vinegar is light in color and has a bright, refreshing flavor. You can find it in well-stocked supermarkets. We use grapeseed oil here for its neutral flavor, but if the only oil you have on hand is olive, the result will still be enjoyable.

Whisk together the shallot, mustard, and vinegar in a small bowl. Slowly drizzle in the oil, whisking to combine, until the vinaigrette is emulsified. Alternatively, you can use a blender. Season to taste with salt and pepper. The vinaigrette will keep in an airtight container in the refrigerator for up to 5 days.

MAKES ABOUT 1 CUP

1 medium shallot, finely chopped

1 teaspoon Dijon mustard

$1/4$ cup white balsamic vinegar

$2/3$ cup grapeseed oil

Salt and freshly ground black pepper

■ warm goat cheese salad

WARM HERBED GOAT CHEESE served over greens dressed with vinaigrette is a bistro classic. We love how we can make the goat cheese disks in advance and bake them for this satisfying salad whenever hunger strikes—which is, of course, often at our ski house.

1. In a small bowl, mix the bread crumbs, thyme, parsley (if using), and pepper. In another small bowl, whisk the egg with the mustard and salt.

2. Cut the goat cheese into 4 equal pieces and press into disks about 3/4 inch thick. Brush the disks with the egg wash and then roll them in the bread crumb mixture, pressing the crumbs gently into the cheese to coat. Place the disks on a small baking sheet and set in the freezer for 15 minutes.

3. Preheat the oven to 450°F.

4. Remove the cheese from the freezer and brush the tops lightly with oil. Transfer to the oven and bake until golden, 10 to 12 minutes.

5. In a large bowl, toss the greens with the vinaigrette to taste. Divide the salad among 4 plates and top each with a goat cheese round. Serve immediately.

SERVES 4

²/₃ cup dried bread crumbs

2 teaspoons chopped fresh thyme or ¹/₂ teaspoon dried

2 teaspoons chopped fresh parsley (optional)

¹/₄ teaspoon freshly ground black pepper

1 large egg

2 teaspoons Dijon mustard

¹/₄ teaspoon salt

6 ounces fresh goat cheese

Extra-virgin olive oil

8 cups baby greens

About ¹/₂ cup Dijon-Balsamic Vinaigrette (page 133)

snowplow salad (the wedge with blue cheese dressing)

IN OUR EXPERIENCE, all skiers start out doing the wedge. This graceless, pigeon-toed stance helps novices get down the mountain in one piece. Then they graduate to a more refined technique.

The same thing has happened to lettuce; our mothers served us iceberg growing up, but now we're fans of all sorts of greens. Since finding good lettuce is often a challenge in winter, especially in grocery stores far from civilization, we fall back on this old-fashioned combination when it is the sensible thing to do. It has a great crunch, especially right out of the refrigerator.

1. To make the dressing: Combine the sour cream, mayonnaise, 1 tablespoon milk, the vinegar, and garlic powder in a medium bowl and stir to combine. Add the blue cheese and stir to combine. Season with salt and pepper to taste. If you prefer a thinner dressing, stir in the remaining 1 tablespoon milk. The dressing will keep in an airtight container in the refrigerator for up to 1 week.

2. To assemble the salad: Remove the outer leaves and core of the lettuce. Slice the head into quarters. Serve the wedges cold, drizzled with dressing and topped with the crumbled bacon and pepper.

SERVES 4

Dressing

$^2/_3$ cup sour cream

$^1/_3$ cup mayonnaise

1 to 2 tablespoons whole milk

2 teaspoons white or red wine vinegar

$^1/_8$ teaspoon garlic powder

1 cup (4 ounces) crumbled blue cheese

Salt and freshly ground black pepper

Salad

1 head iceberg lettuce

4 slices cooked bacon, crumbled

Freshly ground black pepper

sautéed peas with mushrooms and bacon

SOMETIMES, WHILE SKIING IN VERMONT, we find the snow under our skis has the precise texture of frozen peas. This is a problem. However, *actual* frozen peas are one of the most useful items in our freezer. They taste great and cook quickly. (Oh, and in a pinch, an unopened bag of frozen peas makes a great cold compress after a yard sale fall.)

1. In a large skillet over medium heat, cook the bacon until crisp, about 8 minutes. Remove the bacon to drain on paper towels. Reserve 2 table-spoons bacon fat in the pan and return the pan to medium heat.

2. Add the shallot and cook until soft and translucent, about 5 minutes. Add the garlic and cook for 30 seconds. Add the mushrooms and a pinch of salt and pepper and cook for 7 minutes, or until browned and tender.

3. Stir in the peas and cook until heated through, about 2 minutes.

4. Crumble the bacon over the peas. Taste and adjust the seasoning. Serve immediately.

SERVES 6

4 slices thick-cut bacon

1 medium shallot, very thinly sliced

2 garlic cloves, minced

12 ounces white mushrooms, quartered

Salt and freshly ground black pepper

1 (16-ounce) package frozen peas, thawed

sautéed broccoli rabe

BROCCOLI RABE'S SLIGHTLY BITTER TASTE takes to garlic beautifully. Add a tiny hit of peppery heat, and you'll find converts to this healthful vegetable.

1. Trim the coarse stems from the broccoli rabe and discard. Roughly chop the broccoli rabe and set aside.

2. Heat the 3 tablespoons oil in a large skillet over medium heat. Add the garlic and red pepper flakes and cook until the garlic is golden, about 1 minute. Add the broccoli rabe, broth, and a pinch of salt and pepper and toss to coat. Cover and cook until the broccoli rabe is tender, about 5 minutes.

3. Remove the cover, toss, and cook for an additional 2 minutes. Taste and adjust the seasoning. Drizzle with additional oil and serve immediately.

SERVES 4

2 pounds broccoli rabe (about 1 large bunch)

3 tablespoons extra-virgin olive oil, plus more for serving

4 garlic cloves, minced

$1/4$ teaspoon dried red pepper flakes

$1/4$ cup low-sodium chicken broth

Salt and freshly ground black pepper

sautéed spinach with garlic

THIS IS THE ULTIMATE LAST-MINUTE SIDE DISH. What could be easier than opening bags of pre-washed spinach and tossing it with olive oil and garlic for mere minutes? Spinach is a wonderful accompaniment to steak or pork, and it is one of the healthiest vegetables around. The leaves cook down quite a bit, so don't give in to the urge to buy only one bag of leaves, thinking it looks like plenty. You and your fellow diners might be disappointed.

Heat the oil in a large skillet over medium-high heat. Add the garlic and cook until fragrant, about 1 minute. Add the spinach. Cover and cook until the spinach is wilted, tossing frequently, about 3 minutes. Season to taste with salt and pepper. Serve immediately.

SERVES 4

1 tablespoon extra-virgin olive oil

3 garlic cloves, thinly sliced

2 (9-ounce) bags fresh spinach

Salt and freshly ground black pepper

roasted brussels sprouts with bacon

UNFORTUNATELY, 87 PERCENT of the world's Brussels sprouts are served boiled. Okay, we don't know the actual percentage, but we assume it to be high, based on the number of sprout detractors we've met. Roasting Brussels sprouts coaxes out their superb, mellow flavor and texture. Adding bacon gilds the lily.

1. Preheat the oven to 425°F.

2. In a large bowl, toss the Brussels sprouts with the oil, salt, and pepper. Stir in the bacon. Spread on a rimmed baking sheet and roast, stirring once midway through cooking, until the Brussels sprouts are golden brown and cooked through, 25 to 30 minutes. Serve hot.

SERVES 4 TO 6

2 pounds Brussels sprouts, trimmed and cut in half lengthwise

2 tablespoons extra-virgin olive oil

$3/4$ teaspoon salt

$1/4$ teaspoon freshly ground black pepper

4 slices bacon, chopped

● broccoli and bread crumbs

A MOUNTAIN IS BEAUTIFUL all the time, but it looks especially lovely coated with snow, don't you think? We have broccoli quite often, because we like it, but it is an extra treat when it wears a light coating of bread crumbs, which adhere to a bit of garlicky butter. Frozen broccoli makes the dish nearly effortless.

SERVES 4

1 (16-ounce) bag frozen broccoli or broccoli and cauliflower

4 tablespoons butter

3 garlic cloves, minced

3/4 cup store-bought bread crumbs

Salt and freshly ground black pepper

1. Bring 1 cup water to a boil in a medium saucepan. Add the frozen vegetables. Bring the water back to a boil and then reduce the heat so the water simmers. Cover and cook for 5 to 6 minutes, or until the vegetables are tender.

2. Melt the butter over medium heat in a small saucepan. Add the garlic and cook for 1 to 2 minutes, or until the garlic is fragrant and soft. Remove from the heat.

3. Drain the broccoli and then return it to the warm saucepan. Scrape the butter and garlic on top and toss to coat. Stir in the bread crumbs. Season to taste with salt and pepper. Serve immediately in a warmed bowl.

roasted sweet potato fries

SWEET POTATOES, BY DEFINITION, taste sweet. Rather than overwhelming a perfectly good vegetable with brown sugar and marshmallows, we prefer to prepare them as a savory dish. Roasted wedges of sweet potatoes with chili powder are splendid alongside burgers or steaks.

1. Preheat the oven to 450°F.

2. Cut the potatoes in half crosswise and then into $1/2$-inch wedges. In a large bowl, toss the sweet potatoes with the oil, salt, chili powder, and pepper to coat. Arrange the potatoes in a single layer on a rimmed baking sheet. Roast for 30 minutes, turning once midway through cooking, or until the potatoes are tender and golden brown. Serve immediately.

SERVES 4

$1^1/2$ pounds sweet potatoes (about 4 medium)

1 tablespoon extra-virgin olive oil

$3/4$ teaspoon salt

$1/2$ teaspoon chili powder

$1/4$ teaspoon freshly ground black pepper

■ roasted garlic smashed potatoes

MASHED POTATOES ARE AN AMERICAN CLASSIC. As long as they appear on your plate and not on your favorite run, life looks pretty good. We like ours chunky, with the skins on and roasted garlic smashed in.

1. Place the potato chunks in a large pot of cold salted water. Turn the heat to medium-high and bring to a boil. Reduce the heat and simmer for about 15 minutes, or until the potatoes are tender when pierced with a knife. Drain the potatoes and return them to the hot pot.

2. Squeeze the roasted garlic into the potatoes and add the butter and milk. Mash with a potato masher until combined but still chunky. Season to taste with salt and pepper. Serve immediately.

SERVES 6

2½ pounds Yukon Gold potatoes (about 8 medium), cut into large chunks

1 whole head roasted garlic (recipe follows)

¼ cup (½ stick) unsalted butter

½ cup whole milk, half-and-half, or heavy cream

Salt and freshly ground black pepper

roasted garlic

Roasting garlic is one of those amazingly transformative methods. We want to eat the mellow, rich, soft cloves straight out of the papery skins. Add it to soups, pasta, or vegetables, or just eat it smeared on bread. Make extra. Trust us. You'll want more.

1. Preheat the oven to 400°F.
2. Place each garlic head on a sheet of heavy-duty aluminum foil and drizzle with oil. Wrap each head in the foil and place on a baking sheet. Roast for 1 hour.
3. Remove the garlic from the oven, carefully open the foil, and let cool. Squeeze the roasted pulp from the skins and store, covered, in the refrigerator for up to 5 days.

MAKES 4 HEADS ROASTED GARLIC

4 whole heads garlic, top quarters cut off

2 tablespoons extra-virgin olive oil

■ cheesy potato gratin

AN AVALANCHE OF RICH CREAM and cheese makes these spuds into something really divine. And, we're afraid, high in calories; you'd better ski a couple of extra runs—through the trees, no less—tomorrow.

1. Preheat the oven to 375°F. Butter a 9 x 13-inch baking dish.

2. Bring a large pot of salted water to a boil. Add the potatoes and cook for 3 minutes. Drain completely in a colander.

3. Heat the cream, milk, and garlic in a medium saucepan over medium-high heat. Bring to a simmer and then turn off the heat, cover, and let stand for 5 minutes. Discard the garlic and stir in the salt and pepper.

4. Place one-third of the potato slices in the baking dish, overlapping them to form a single layer. Sprinkle with ½ cup of the cheese. Repeat with another layer of potatoes and cheese. Finish with a layer of potatoes. Pour the cream mixture over the potatoes and then sprinkle with the remaining 1 cup cheese.

5. Bake for 35 minutes, or until the potatoes are tender and the top is golden brown.

SERVES 8

Unsalted butter

2½ pounds russet potatoes, peeled and very thinly sliced

1½ cups heavy cream

1 cup whole milk

2 garlic cloves, peeled and sliced in half

¾ teaspoon salt

¼ teaspoon freshly ground black pepper

2 cups (8 ounces) grated Gruyère

● roasted potatoes with rosemary

THESE CRISP BROWN WEDGES are a great last-minute accompaniment to any meat. They are so companionable, in fact, that you can go ahead and cook them at any temperature between 350° and 425°F; just vary the cooking time accordingly. These are simpler to prepare than mashed potatoes, but just as satisfying. You can also pass them off to your children as French fries. Don't forget the ketchup.

---

1. Preheat the oven to 400°F.

2. In a large bowl, toss the potatoes with the oil, rosemary, and salt and pepper to taste. Spread the wedges on a rimmed baking sheet.

3. Tossing the wedges halfway through, roast for 30 minutes, or until tender when pierced with a knife and well browned. Serve immediately.

SERVES 4 TO 6

2^1/$_2$ pounds Yukon Gold or russet potatoes, halved and cut into ^{1}/$_2$-inch wedges

3 tablespoons olive oil

1 tablespoon chopped fresh rosemary or 1 teaspoon dried

Salt and freshly ground black pepper

■ vermont risotto

CREAMY RISOTTO is a wonderful comfort food. Traditionally flavored with Parmesan cheese, risotto gets an American twist here with a sprinkling of aged Cheddar instead. We particularly like two-year-old Grafton, made in Grafton, Vermont.

---

1. Heat the broth in a medium saucepan until it simmers.

2. Meanwhile, heat the oil and butter in a large pot over medium heat. Add the onion and cook for 5 minutes, or until soft and fragrant. Add the rice and stir for 3 minutes.

3. Add the vinegar and cook, stirring, until the liquid is nearly absorbed. Add the broth $1/4$ cup at a time, maintaining a slow simmer. Stir frequently and allow each addition of liquid to be absorbed before adding the next. The risotto will be done about 35 minutes after the vinegar is added. Taste the dish for texture—if the rice is soft, the cooking is complete. Otherwise, add another $1/4$ cup water and continue to simmer until the texture is right.

4. Remove from the heat. Stir in the Cheddar and salt and pepper to taste. Serve immediately.

NOTE To turn this side dish into a meal, stir in 2 cups sautéed mushrooms or 1 cup each cubed leftover cooked chicken and thawed frozen peas.

SERVES 4

1 ($14^1/_2$-ounce) can low-sodium chicken broth

1 tablespoon olive oil

1 tablespoon unsalted butter

$1/2$ small onion, finely minced

1 cup Arborio rice

$1/4$ cup white balsamic vinegar or dry white wine

1 cup (4 ounces) shredded sharp or extra-sharp Cheddar

Salt and freshly ground black pepper

● buttermilk corn bread

THIS VERSION OF CORN BREAD is sturdy, not sweet. Pair it with chili or other hearty dishes. Use this basic recipe as the perfect launching point for a spicy, chile-Cheddar version, or simply serve it plain, toasted, or with jam for breakfast.

---

1. Preheat the oven to 425°F. Butter an 8 x 8-inch baking pan and set aside.

2. In a large bowl, whisk together the flour, cornmeal, baking powder, baking soda, and salt. In a medium bowl, whisk together the egg, buttermilk, sugar, and melted butter. Mix the wet ingredients into the dry ingredients and stir to just combine; do not overmix.

3. Pour the batter into the prepared pan and bake for 20 minutes, or until golden and a toothpick inserted into the center comes out clean.

4. Remove from the oven and let cool at least 10 minutes before serving. The corn bread will keep, in the baking pan, wrapped with plastic wrap or foil, for up to 3 days at room temperature.

✳ CHILE CHEDDAR CORN BREAD

Add to the batter 1 cup shredded sharp Cheddar, 1 cup defrosted frozen corn kernels, and 1 (4½-ounce) can green chiles, drained, 1 minced jalapeño, or 3 to 4 canned chipotle peppers in adobo, drained and chopped.

MAKES 9 (2-INCH) PIECES

1 cup all-purpose flour

1 cup yellow cornmeal

1 tablespoon baking powder

½ teaspoon baking soda

¼ teaspoon salt

1 large egg

1¼ cups buttermilk

3 tablespoons sugar

4 tablespoons (½ stick) unsalted butter, melted and cooled, plus more for the pan

● couscous with currants

UNLIKE RICE OR WHOLE GRAINS, couscous cooks fully in eight minutes, making it an extremely handy dish to keep on hand. Pair it with a fast food entrée, and you can get your skis sharpened after the lifts close and still make dinner for the family. This dish is nice served warm, but it also works as a cold salad, a great accompaniment to leftovers, or lunch.

1. In a medium saucepan over medium heat, melt the butter. Add the scallion whites and carrots and cook for 2 to 3 minutes, or until the vegetables are soft.

2. Add the couscous and stir to blend with the butter and vegetables. Add the broth. Bring the mixture to a boil. Reduce the heat to low and simmer, covered, for 7 to 8 minutes, or until all of the liquid is absorbed. Let stand off the heat, covered, for 5 minutes.

3. Transfer the couscous to a serving bowl and fluff with a fork. Stir in the scallion greens, salt, and currants. Serve warm, at room temperature, or cold. The couscous can be covered and refrigerated for up to 3 days.

SERVES 6

3 tablespoons unsalted butter

1 large or 2 small bunches scallions (about 8), white and green parts chopped separately

2 medium carrots, grated

2 cups whole wheat couscous

4 cups low-sodium chicken broth

$1/2$ teaspoon salt

$1/2$ cup dried currants

● homemade applesauce

THE TASTE OF FRESH APPLESAUCE alongside a pork or chicken dish is so much livelier than anything that comes out of a jar. And don't even get us started on how amazing this makes your house smell while it cooks! While any tart apple will do, including Cortland, Paula Red, or Macoun, even grocery store Granny Smith apples will produce a superior applesauce with minimal effort on your part.

---

1. Place the apples, cinnamon, lemon zest (if using), sugar, and $1/4$ cup water in a large saucepan over medium-low heat. Simmer for 20 minutes, or until the apples are falling apart.

2. Discard the cinnamon stick and lemon zest. Mash the apple mixture with a potato masher or fork.

3. Serve warm or at room temperature as an accompaniment to meat, or serve cold as a snack. The applesauce can be covered and refrigerated for up to 3 days or, once cooled, frozen for up to 1 month.

NOTE You can also make the applesauce in a microwave oven. Toss the apples, cinnamon, lemon zest, and sugar in a microwave-safe dish and cover loosely with plastic wrap. Place in the microwave and cook at full power for 5 minutes. Stir to combine and then cook for $1^1/2$ minutes more, or until the apples mash easily with a fork. Discard the cinnamon stick and lemon zest before serving.

MAKES ABOUT $2^1/_2$ CUPS

6 small or 4 large tart apples, cored, peeled, and thinly sliced (about 5 cups)

1 (3-inch) cinnamon stick or $1/_2$ teaspoon ground cinnamon

1 strip lemon zest (optional)

1 tablespoon brown sugar

desserts

WE'VE EARNED IT. Some of us earned it carving off-piste through the trees or tackling the steepest mogul run under the lift. Some of us earned it by toting all of our gear plus the gear for three children to the hill and then back again. For venturing into the frozen world while others stayed at home parked in front of the television, and for barreling down a vertical drop of 2,800 feet again and again and again, we've earned it.

And because we've earned it, we don't want to work too hard for it. In this chapter, we offer satisfying treats that aren't fussy. You'll find fudgy brownies, Chocolate Chip Pan Cookies, and Peanut Butter Cookies. All of them are a snap to make.

If you're not into baking, try either caramel or hot fudge sauce for ice cream, or chocolate fondue, which is about as no-fail as a recipe can be. In fact, if we were going to vote on the recipe with the greatest impact for the least effort, chocolate fondue would win. Can anyone resist fruit dipped into molten chocolate?

For a showstopper dessert, replicate the amazing Sticky Toffee Pudding from Sweet Basil in Vail, Colorado. We turn to poached pears when we want to make a similarly elegant finish to a meal.

If your ski house is nestled high in the mountains and your favorite baking recipes are proving problematic, consult our appendix on high-altitude cooking and baking (page 180) for tips on adjusting recipes in elevation.

fabulously fudgy cocoa brownies

TINA AND HER SISTER have never agreed on whether the family recipe for their easy, moist, and chocolaty brownies should be given out. Here we settle the question and satisfy friends who have begged for the recipe for years. These brownies are so easy to stir together, we wonder why anyone would ever bother buying a mix again.

1. Preheat the oven to 350°F.

2. In a small saucepan over low heat, gently melt the butter with the cocoa, stirring frequently until thoroughly combined. Set aside to cool.

3. In a medium bowl, combine the sugar, eggs, and vanilla. Stir with a wooden spoon until the mixture is well blended and pale yellow in color. Add the cooled chocolate mixture and stir to combine. Add the flour and salt and stir just to combine.

4. Pour the mixture into an 8-inch square baking pan and bake for 20 to 25 minutes, or until cooked through but still moist in the center. A toothpick inserted into the center should have crumbs clinging to it.

5. Cool in the pan for at least 15 minutes before cutting into bars. Serve warm or at room temperature. The brownies will keep in the baking pan, wrapped with plastic wrap or foil, for 3 to 4 days at room temperature.

BROWNIES PLUS

For variety, add one or two of the following with the chocolate mixture in step 3.

$1/4$ teaspoon cayenne

$1/4$ teaspoon ground cinnamon

1 tablespoon instant espresso powder

1 cup chocolate chunks or chips

1 cup chopped toasted nuts, such as walnuts or pecans

MAKES 16 (2-INCH) SQUARES

8 tablespoons (1 stick) unsalted butter

$1/2$ cup unsweetened cocoa powder

$1^1/4$ cups sugar

2 large eggs

$3/4$ teaspoon vanilla extract

$3/4$ cup all-purpose flour

$1/4$ teaspoon salt

● chocolate chip pan cookies

WE HATE BAKING COOKIES IN BATCHES. The first batch is great, but waiting for the sheet to cool and then starting over quickly loses its charm. And when we try to cram too many cookies into one batch, they run together in the oven. The solution? *Deliberately* running the cookies together. Instead of baking batch after batch of cookies, we're kickin' back by the fire.

1. Preheat the oven to 350°F. Butter an 11 x 17-inch rimmed baking sheet and set aside.

2. In a medium bowl, stir together the flour, oats, baking powder, baking soda, and salt.

3. In a large bowl, combine both sugars and the butter. Add the eggs and stir briskly with a wooden spoon to combine. Add the vanilla and stir to combine. Stir in the dry ingredients, followed by the chocolate chips and nuts, if desired.

4. Drop the batter in 3 or 4 mounds onto the baking sheet. Use the back of a wooden spoon to flatten and spread the batter as evenly as possible over the pan. Bake for 10 minutes, rotate the pan, and bake for another 3 to 5 minutes, or until the surface of the cookie is evenly golden brown.

5. Cool on a rack for at least 10 minutes. Cut the cookie into bars and serve at room temperature. The cookies will keep in the baking pan, wrapped with plastic wrap or foil, for 3 to 4 days at room temperature.

MAKES 30 LARGE BAR COOKIES

2 cups all-purpose flour

1/2 cup old-fashioned rolled oats

1 teaspoon baking powder

1 teaspoon baking soda

1/2 teaspoon salt

1 1/2 cups (packed) light brown sugar

1/4 cup granulated sugar

1 cup (2 sticks) unsalted butter, melted and cooled, plus more for the pan

2 large eggs

1 tablespoon vanilla extract

1 (12-ounce) package (2 cups) semisweet chocolate chips

1 cup chopped pecans (optional)

● peanut butter cookies

SOMETIMES YOU WANT A SWEET TREAT...fast! And there's nothing like a cookie hot out of the oven. These peanut butter cookies have just five ingredients, which expedites the hand-to-mouth experience.

MAKES 24 COOKIES

1 cup peanut butter

1 cup sugar

1 large egg, lightly beaten

2 tablespoons all-purpose flour

1 teaspoon baking soda

1. Preheat the oven to 350°F.

2. In a large bowl, mix together the peanut butter, sugar, egg, flour, and baking soda until thoroughly combined. Roll rounded teaspoonfuls of the dough into balls and place on baking sheets, about 1 inch apart. With the tines of a fork, flatten the balls, making a criss-cross pattern.

3. Bake until the cookies are puffed and lightly golden, 8 to 10 minutes. Cool on the baking sheets for 2 minutes before removing to racks to cool completely. The cookies will keep in a cookie jar or sealed container for up to 5 days at room temperature.

■ snowy peaks (chocolate-dipped coconut macaroons)

THIS SUPER-EASY COOKIE has a haystack shape that reminds us of our favorite ski hills. The combination of sweet coconut and bittersweet chocolate will have everyone asking for more.

1. Preheat the oven to 350°F.

2. In a large bowl, whisk the egg whites until frothy. Add the sugar, vanilla, and salt. Stir to combine. Add the coconut and mix well, completely combining the ingredients.

3. Dampen your hands with cold water. Form a rounded tablespoon of the mixture into a haystack shape and place on a nonstick baking sheet. Repeat with the remaining mixture, spacing the stacks about 1 inch apart.

4. Bake until golden brown, about 18 minutes, rotating the sheet halfway through baking. Remove the cookies from the pan while still hot to cool completely on racks.

5. Fill a small saucepan with water to a depth of 1 inch and bring to a boil. Reduce the heat to low and place a medium heatproof bowl on top so the bottom is resting on the pan just above the water. Add the chocolate and stir until completely melted.

6. Turn off the heat and dip each macaroon bottom into the melted chocolate. Place on wax paper to cool and harden. The macaroons can be stored in an airtight container for up to 2 days or refrigerated for up to 5 days.

MAKES ABOUT 36 COOKIES

4 large egg whites

¼ cup sugar

1 teaspoon vanilla extract

Pinch of salt

1 (14-ounce) package shredded sweetened coconut (about 5⅓ cups)

4 ounces bittersweet chocolate bar, chopped (about 1 cup)

● gingerbread

THE SMELL OF GINGERBREAD baking in the oven is a distinctly winter aroma. Although we're not fans of rolling out gingerbread cookie dough, we do enjoy a simple gingerbread cake. It's just as good for dessert, a snack, or breakfast.

1. Preheat the oven to 350°F. Butter a 9-inch round cake pan and set aside.

2. In a medium bowl, whisk together the flour, ginger, cinnamon, cocoa, cloves, baking soda, and salt. In a large bowl, whisk together the egg, molasses, brown sugar, and oil. Add the dry ingredients to the wet ingredients and whisk together. Add the boiling water and stir to combine.

3. Pour the batter into the prepared pan and bake for 40 to 45 minutes, or until a toothpick inserted into the center comes out clean. Let cool for at least 15 minutes before slicing.

4. Serve warm or at room temperature. If you've cooled the cake completely, you can garnish it with a sprinkling of powdered sugar, if desired. The cake will keep in the baking pan, wrapped with plastic wrap or foil, for up to 5 days at room temperature.

MAKES 1 (9-INCH) CAKE

Unsalted butter

2 cups all-purpose flour

2 teaspoons ground ginger

1 teaspoon ground cinnamon

1 teaspoon unsweetened cocoa powder

$1/4$ teaspoon ground cloves

$1/2$ teaspoon baking soda

$1/4$ teaspoon salt

1 large egg

$3/4$ cup molasses

$1/2$ cup plus 1 tablespoon (packed) light brown sugar

$1/2$ cup vegetable oil

1 cup boiling water

Powdered sugar (optional)

♦ sticky toffee pudding

WE DEVOURED THIS DELICIOUSLY DECADENT DESSERT the first time we tasted it. In our sugar haze (or maybe it was the wine), we declared that we could make it at home. Fortunately for all of us, Sweet Basil, a dining destination in Vail, Colorado, was willing to share their recipe. We've tweaked it for the home cook, and we know you'll be pleased. The evidence: empty (but sticky) dish.

1. Preheat the oven to 325°F. Butter an 8 x 12-inch baking dish and set aside.

2. Put the dates in a medium saucepan and cover with water. Place over high heat and bring to a boil. Cook for 3 minutes, remove from the heat, strain, and cool. When the dates are cool enough to handle, peel and chop them.

3. Return the dates to the saucepan and add 2 cups water. Bring to a boil and remove from the heat. Stir in the baking soda and vanilla. (The mixture will bubble up and foam.) Set aside to cool.

4. Whisk together the flour, baking powder, and salt in a medium bowl. Mix the butter and sugar together in a large bowl until light and fluffy. Add the eggs and stir until well blended. Alternately add the date mixture and the flour mixture to the eggs in 3 additions, stirring after each until the batter is smooth and well combined.

5. Pour the batter into the prepared dish and bake for 40 to 45 minutes, or until brown and a skewer inserted into the center comes out clean. Cut the baked pudding into 12 squares, but do not remove them from the dish.

SERVES 12

Cake

2 cups pitted dates (10 ounces)

2 teaspoons baking soda

2 teaspoons vanilla

2 cups all-purpose flour

1 teaspoon baking powder

1/4 teaspoon salt

8 tablespoons (1 stick) unsalted butter, softened, plus more for the baking dish

1 1/2 cups sugar

3 large eggs

Toffee Sauce

8 tablespoons (1 stick) unsalted butter

1 (16-ounce) box light brown sugar

2 cups heavy cream

2 tablespoons dark rum or brandy (optional)

6. To make the toffee sauce: While the cake is baking, melt the butter and brown sugar in a large saucepan over medium heat. Cook, stirring, until the butter is melted and the sugar is dissolved, about 7 minutes. Stir in the cream and bring the mixture to a boil. (Watch the pot carefully, making sure it doesn't boil over.) Remove from the heat and stir in the rum, if desired.

7. Pour half of the sauce over the baked pudding, allowing it to seep down into it. Return the dish to the oven and bake for 5 minutes more.

8. Remove from the oven and let cool for 10 minutes. Serve immediately, topped with the remaining sauce.

• chocolate fondue

THIS IS A CAN'T-MISS FAMILY and crowd favorite. All the preparation takes place at the grocery store, where you stock up on chocolate and dipping treats. We like to use a chocolate of about 70 percent cacao for this recipe, but we're pretty hard-core. Any good chocolate with at least 55 percent cacao will taste divine.

SERVES 6

1/2 cup heavy cream

12 ounces bittersweet chocolate, chopped (about 3 cups)

1 tablespoon honey

1 tablespoon kirsch (optional)

Fruit, cookies, or other treats for dipping, such as 2 bananas, halved lengthwise and cut into 1-inch pieces; 2 oranges, peeled and separated into sections; 2 apples, thinly sliced; shortbread cookies, gingersnaps, or graham crackers; pound cake, cut into 1-inch chunks; or marshmallows

1. In a medium saucepan over medium heat, bring the cream to a simmer. Turn off the heat and add the chocolate. Wait for 5 minutes, and then whisk to combine.

2. Stir in the honey and kirsch, if desired. Transfer the contents to a fondue pot set over a very low flame. Serve immediately with a platter of fruit, cookies, or other treats and fondue forks or skewers for dipping.

■ milk chocolate bread pudding

SOME SKI LOCALES ARE FAMOUS for their snow texture; there is the champagne powder of Colorado and the infamous Sierra cement. Puddings also have distinctive textures. There is the classic creamy chocolate pudding, the slightly more textured rice pudding, and of course Sticky Toffee Pudding, which isn't really a pudding at all. Bread pudding falls somewhere in between. While it certainly is not velvety smooth, it is a scrumptious way to use up stale bread.

---

1. Combine the milk, cream, and vanilla in a medium saucepan over medium-high heat. Bring to a simmer and then turn off the heat. Add the chocolate, let stand for 3 minutes, and then whisk until smooth.

2. In a large bowl, whisk the whole eggs, egg yolks, sugar, and hazelnut liqueur to combine. Very gradually add the hot cream mixture, whisking constantly.

3. Preheat the oven to 325°F. Butter a 9 x 13-inch baking dish.

4. Add the bread to the chocolate mixture and toss to coat completely. Pour the mixture into the prepared dish and allow to stand for 20 minutes. Bake until set and browning on top, about 45 minutes. Serve warm or at room temperature. Store covered and refrigerated for up to 3 days.

SERVES 8

2 cups whole milk

2 cups heavy cream

2 teaspoons vanilla extract

1 pound milk chocolate, chopped (about 4 cups)

4 large eggs

4 large egg yolks

1/3 cup sugar

3 tablespoons hazelnut liqueur, such as Frangelico

Unsalted butter

1 loaf brioche or Pullman bread, cut into 1-inch cubes (about 12 cups)

■ carrot cake
with cream cheese frosting

DOES THE NON-SKIING WORLD know what a truly useful word *dump* is? As in "I'm heading to the mountain, dude, because it seriously dumped last night." Or what about dump cakes? Our friend Norm's carrot cake is such a cake. You simply dump the dry ingredients into the wet ingredients, stir together, and then bake. There is no sifting, no gentle folding, no whipping egg whites. After enjoying the dumping outside, revel in this dump cake inside.

---

1. Preheat the oven to 350°F. Butter 2 (9-inch) round cake pans.

2. To make the cake: In a medium bowl, stir together the flour, sugar, baking powder, baking soda, cinnamon, nutmeg, and salt. In a large bowl, beat the eggs lightly to combine, and then whisk in the oil. Add the dry ingredients to the wet ingredients and stir to combine. Stir in the carrots, pecans, and raisins, if using.

3. Divide the batter evenly between the prepared pans. Bake for 30 to 35 minutes, or until a toothpick inserted into the center of the cakes comes out clean. Remove to a rack to cool for 5 minutes, then unmold and cool completely.

4. To make the frosting: In a large bowl, beat together the cream cheese, confectioners' sugar, butter, and vanilla. Spread the frosting between the layers and over the sides and top of the cake. Store, covered, at room temperature for up to 2 days or refrigerated for up to 5 days.

NOTE For an even simpler presentation, bake the batter in a 9 x 13-inch pan for 45 minutes and simply frost the top.

MAKES 1 (9-INCH) LAYER CAKE

Cake

Unsalted butter

2 cups all-purpose flour

2 cups sugar

2 teaspoons baking powder

2 teaspoons baking soda

2 teaspoons ground cinnamon

Pinch of ground nutmeg

1 teaspoon salt

4 large eggs

1⅓ cups canola oil

3 cups shredded carrots (about 6 medium)

1 cup chopped pecans

½ cup raisins (optional)

Frosting

1 (8-ounce) package cream cheese, room temperature

1 (16-ounce) box confectioners' sugar

8 tablespoons (1 stick) unsalted butter, softened

2 teaspoons vanilla extract

● apple crisp

NOTHING IS MORE COMFORTING than the smell of apples baking with cinnamon. This dessert is a good one for putting into the oven just as you sit down to eat dinner. When the dishes are done, you can sit down again with your apple crisp and linger over dessert. Use a variety of apples to mix up the flavor and texture. We are also occasionally guilty of doubling the crumble topping for an extra-crunchy apple crisp.

1. Preheat the oven to 350°F.

2. Combine the butter, flour, and $1/2$ cup of the sugar in a medium bowl. Use a pastry blender or 2 knives to cut the mixture together until crumbly. Set aside.

3. Place the apples in a 2-quart baking dish. Sprinkle with the cinnamon, salt, and remaining $1/4$ cup sugar and stir to combine. Top evenly with the crumb mixture.

4. Bake until bubbly and the apples are soft, about 40 minutes. Serve warm with vanilla ice cream.

SERVES 6

4 tablespoons ($1/2$ stick) unsalted butter

$1/2$ cup all-purpose flour

$3/4$ cup sugar

6 large apples (about 3 pounds), cored, peeled, and thickly sliced

$1/4$ teaspoon ground cinnamon

Pinch of salt

Vanilla ice cream

■ red wine–poached pears

SOMETIMES WE WANT SOMETHING a little sweet after dinner, but less sweet than a cake or pie. Poaching pears in red wine and spices infuses them with flavor without adding loads of extra calories. The beautiful color the wine imparts makes for a particularly impressive dessert. Your friends don't have to know how easy it was to make.

SERVES 4

4 ripe but firm pears

1 (750-ml) bottle red wine

1 cup sugar

2 (3-inch) cinnamon sticks

1 bay leaf

1 vanilla bean, split lengthwise

1. Peel the pears. Using a paring knife, core them from the bottom, leaving the stems intact. Make a thin slice across the bottom of each pear to form a flat surface on which the pear can stand.

2. In a large saucepan, combine the wine, 1 cup water, the sugar, cinnamon sticks, bay leaf, and vanilla bean and bring to a boil over high heat. Reduce the heat and add the pears. Simmer, uncovered, until the pears are tender, about 35 minutes. Remove from the heat and cool the pears in the poaching liquid. At this point, the pears can be refrigerated in their liquid for up to 2 days.

3. To serve, remove the pears from the poaching liquid and set them aside. Strain the liquid into a large saucepan and bring to a boil over high heat. Reduce the heat to medium and continue cooking until the liquid is reduced by half, 35 to 40 minutes. Cool to room temperature.

4. Serve the pears, drizzled with the reduced poaching liquid.

◆ rustic apple-pear pie

FREESTYLE SKIING LETS YOU SHOW OFF your own style. Without a pie plate to confine you, a free-form pie can do the same. We love just rolling out the dough and assembling this pie on a sheet pan, thus easily impressing your friends.

1. To make the crust: Mix the flour, 1 tablespoon of the granulated sugar, and salt in a large bowl. Add the butter. Using a pastry blender or 2 knives, cut the butter into the flour mixture until crumbly.

2. In a small bowl, mix the ice water with the egg yolk. Add to the flour mixture. Stir just until a dough forms. (Add another 1 tablespoon water if the dough is too dry to hold together.) Gather the dough into a ball and flatten into a disk. Wrap in plastic wrap and refrigerate until firm, at least 1 hour or up to 1 day.

3. To make the topping: Mix the walnuts, flour, brown sugar, and cinnamon in a medium bowl. Add the butter and, using a pastry blender, cut it in until the mixture is crumbly.

4. Preheat the oven to 375°F.

5. To make the filling: In a large bowl, mix the apples, pears, granulated sugar, flour, and lemon juice until combined.

6. Roll out the dough to a 13-inch round. Transfer to a large baking sheet. Spoon the fruit mixture over the dough, mounding it in the center and leaving a 2-inch border. Fold the dough border partially over the filling to form a 9-inch round. Top the exposed fruit filling with the crumb topping. Whisk the remaining egg with 2 teaspoons water to make an egg wash. Brush the crust with the egg wash and sprinkle with the remaining tablespoon granulated sugar.

7. Bake the pie until the crust is golden and the fruit is tender, rotating halfway through baking, about 50 minutes. Transfer the baking sheet to a rack to cool for 15 minutes. Serve at room temperature.

SERVES 10

Crust
1½ cups all-purpose flour

2 tablespoons granulated sugar

¼ teaspoon salt

10 tablespoons unsalted butter, cold, cut into pieces

3 tablespoons ice water

1 large egg yolk

1 large egg

Crumb Topping
¾ cup chopped walnuts

¾ cup all-purpose flour

⅔ cup (packed) light brown sugar

½ teaspoon ground cinnamon

8 tablespoons (1 stick) unsalted butter, cold, cut into pieces

Filling
2 medium apples, peeled, cored, and cut into ¼-inch wedges

2 medium ripe but firm pears, peeled, cored, and cut into ¼-inch wedges

⅓ cup granulated sugar

¼ cup all-purpose flour

1 tablespoon fresh lemon juice

● hot fudge sauce

THERE IS ABSOLUTELY NO REASON why you should not enjoy ice cream in the winter. The state with the highest per capita ice cream consumption is Minnesota, where it snows plenty. If you're like us, you get that fireplace cranked up a little too high and end up opening the windows anyway. Get out the ice cream and stir together this simple hot fudge, a childhood favorite of Tina's.

MAKES ABOUT 2 CUPS

4 ounces bittersweet chocolate, chopped (about 1 cup)

2 tablespoons unsalted butter

1 (14-ounce) can sweetened condensed milk

1 teaspoon vanilla extract

Pinch of salt

Ice cream

---

1. Gently melt the chocolate and butter together in a small saucepan over low heat, stirring frequently.

2. Add the milk, vanilla, and salt to the chocolate mixture and stir to combine. Cook for 5 minutes, or until hot and slightly thickened. Serve immediately over ice cream. Store for up to 3 weeks in a tightly sealed container or glass jar in the refrigerator. Reheat gently over low heat, stirring frequently, or in the microwave on high, stirring every 20 seconds until heated through.

MOCHA HOT FUDGE SAUCE

Prepare Hot Fudge Sauce, above, adding 1 tablespoon instant espresso powder in step 1.

■ caramel sauce

WE EAT THIS CARAMEL SAUCE drizzled over apples, ice cream, pie, bread pudding, brownies, popcorn ... It's also incredibly simple to make as long as you are patient enough to watch it. The color changes from golden to amber quickly, and the sugar can burn before you know it. After you make this sauce once, you'll know why we also eat it right off a spoon.

1^1/$_3$ cups sugar

^{1}/$_2$ cup heavy cream

^{1}/$_2$ teaspoon vanilla extract

1 tablespoon unsalted butter

---

1. Set ^{1}/$_2$ cup water in a medium saucepan over medium-high heat. Pour the sugar into the middle of the pan. Bring to a boil and cook until the mixture is thick and golden, 7 to 8 minutes. Do not stir.

2. Reduce the heat to medium and continue to cook until the mixture is amber in color, 1 to 2 minutes.

3. Turn off the heat and slowly pour in the cream, taking care, as the hot mixture will bubble vigorously. Add the vanilla and whisk until combined. Add the butter and whisk until melted and smooth. Serve warm.

NOTE This sauce can be refrigerated in a tightly sealed container for up to 1 month. Reheat gently over low heat or in the microwave on high, stirring every 20 seconds until heated through.

beverages

HYDRATION IS IMPORTANT FOR SKIERS. Even in cold weather, you can work up a good sweat on the hill, and altitude is an additional robber of moisture from the body. For these reasons, we'd like to remind you to drink plenty of water while you ski or ride.

Now that we've got that out of the way, let's talk about beverages—the ones to enjoy après-ski. We have four mixed cocktails we're never without. While Cognac is one of our favorite wintertime liquors, we like it in mixed drinks as opposed to neat. The sidecar is, in our humble opinion, a fine traditional cocktail that hasn't had its due. We also like a sour cherry twist on the martini and a classic margarita for those nights when we've made a hearty Mexican feast.

The frigid weather provides a great excuse to whip up hot beverages, with or without alcohol. We include two versions of hot cocoa—a quick cocoa and a richer hot chocolate. Choose between them on the basis of the ingredients you have on hand. Both are infinitely superior to the bland, sugary stuff that comes out of the machines at most ski lodges.

The traditional hot toddy, a drink that seems to make it into a lot of old movies but not into our mugs, is nothing but whiskey and hot water. The Cranberry Cosmo-Toddy is our tasty update with cranberry juice and rum. We also do hot cider, hot buttered rum, and a glögg recipe that will warm you all the way to your toes.

Cheers!

● sidecar

IF YOU LIKE COSMOPOLITANS in the summer, the classic sidecar just might become your wintertime cocktail. The rich Cognac flavor is well suited to the season. Rimming the glass with sugar plays up the balance of sweet and sour.

1. Rim the edge of a martini glass with lemon juice and sugar (see Note).

2. Pour the Cognac, Cointreau, and lemon juice into a cocktail shaker filled with ice cubes. Shake briskly and strain into the martini glass. Garnish with lemon zest.

NOTE To rim a glass, dip its rim into a plate of lemon juice and then into a plate of sugar (or salt).

MAKES 1 DRINK

Lemon juice

Sugar

1½ ounces (3 tablespoons) Cognac or brandy

1 ounce (2 tablespoons) Cointreau or other orange-flavored liqueur

1 ounce (2 tablespoons) fresh lemon juice

1 strip lemon zest

● cognac and tonic

WHILE MOST TONIC DRINKS are downright summery, Cognac is so rich this version works all year round. Use VS or VSOP Cognac, not the fancy stuff. Even if you think this combination sounds a bit odd, try it. Trust us: The refreshing blend is better than the sum of its parts. Just think—a decade or so ago, some guy decided to try strapping both his feet to a skateboard and surfing down the mountain. People thought that was a weird combination too.

MAKES 1 DRINK

2 ounces (¼ cup) Cognac

2 lime wedges

6 ounces (¾ cup) tonic water

Pour the Cognac into a highball glass filled with ice cubes. Squeeze a wedge of lime over the ice. Top with the tonic water and stir. Garnish with the remaining wedge of lime.

margarita

IT'S A SHAME that you can't ski in Mexico—but you *can* shake up the classic margarita above 3,000 feet without a problem. With the right ingredients and a cocktail shaker, you'll be imagining warm ocean breezes even if your northern weather is 10 below.

1. Rim the edge of a martini glass with lime juice and salt (see Note, page 172).

2. Pour the tequila, Cointreau, fresh lime juice, and Rose's lime juice into a cocktail shaker filled with ice cubes. Shake briskly and strain into the martini glass. Garnish with the lime wedge.

MAKES 1 DRINK

Lime juice

Salt

1¹/₂ ounces (3 tablespoons) tequila

1 ounce (2 tablespoons) Cointreau or other orange-flavored liqueur

1 ounce (2 tablespoons) fresh lime juice

Dash of Rose's lime juice

1 lime wedge

sour cherrytini

WE'RE FROM MICHIGAN, where they grow a lot of tasty sour cherries. And while it snows a lot there, the vertical drop of the tallest ski hill in the Lower Peninsula is 550 feet. To bring a little of our home state spirit to our ski house, we make these sour cherry cocktails. Sour cherry concentrate can be purchased at www.cherryrepublic.com, or you can substitute regular cherry juice.

1. Rim the edge of a martini glass with lime juice and sugar (see Note, page 172).

2. Pour the vodka, Cointreau, lime juice, and sour cherry concentrate into a cocktail shaker filled with ice cubes. Shake briskly and strain into the martini glass.

MAKES 1 DRINK

Lime juice

Sugar

1¹/₂ ounces (3 tablespoons) citrus vodka

1 ounce (2 tablespoons) Cointreau or other orange-flavored liqueur

1 ounce (2 tablespoons) fresh lime juice

2 teaspoons sour cherry concentrate

• cranberry cosmo-toddy

LIGHTER THAN BUTTERED RUM, crisper than mulled wine, and nicely acidic, this is the hot drink for people who think they don't like hot drinks. Enjoy a little rum with your vitamin C.

Heat the cranberry juice and the orange and lemon slices in a medium saucepan over medium-high heat. Bring to a simmer. Turn off the heat and stir in the rum. Serve immediately.

SERVES 4

1 (32-ounce) bottle cranberry juice cocktail

1 orange, sliced

1 lemon, sliced

1 cup dark rum

■ glögg

FIRST OF ALL, *glögg* rhymes with *chug*. Second, glögg is a beverage more traditional to Norse woodsmen than to skiers, but it is traditional cold-weather fare all the same, and delicious, so why split hairs? While stronger than mulled wine, glögg has the same fragrant spiciness. And because of all of the flavorful enhancements you'll be adding, feel free to select an inexpensive wine.

1. In a small bowl, combine the vodka, cloves, cardamom, cinnamon sticks, ginger, and orange zest. Set aside for at least 1 hour, or covered for up to 1 week.

2. Combine the wine and sugar in a large saucepan. Bring to a boil, reduce the heat, and simmer until the sugar is dissolved, about 5 minutes. Add the vodka mixture and return to a simmer.

3. Strain and serve warm.

SERVES 6

1½ cups vodka

10 cloves

10 cardamom pods

2 (3-inch) cinnamon sticks

1 (2-inch) piece fresh ginger, peeled

Zest of 1 orange

1 (750-ml) bottle inexpensive red
 wine

½ cup sugar

HOT
COCOA

MOGUL MINT
MOCHA

● hot cocoa

THOUGH IT TAKES ONLY A FEW MINUTES to make, this classic beverage is superior to anything you dump out of an envelope into your cup. Creating a cocoa paste aids in dissolving the sugar, minimizes lumps, and increases the frothiness after the scalded milk is added.

MAKES 1 DRINK

1 tablespoon unsweetened cocoa powder

4 teaspoons sugar

1 cup whole milk

Marshmallows (optional)

1. In a mug, stir together the cocoa powder, sugar, and 2 teaspoons of the milk to form a paste.

2. In a small saucepan over medium-high heat, bring the remaining milk to a boil. Just as it reaches the boil, remove from the heat and slowly stir into the mug containing the cocoa mixture. Stir until incorporated and frothy. Serve immediately, topped with marshmallows, if desired.

✳ QUICK CAFÉ MOCHA

We find, among our circle of friends, that chocolate addiction and caffeine addiction often occur in the same people. To please them (and ourselves), we prepare Hot Cocoa, above, adding 1 to 2 teaspoons instant espresso powder to the mug in step 1.

● rich hot chocolate

WE MAKE OUR RICH HOT CHOCOLATE with chips, both for ease of melting and the smooth texture they impart. This recipe is for everyone who skied in weather so cold they had to wear face masks with openings only for their nostrils and eyes. Or, really, for anyone.

Combine the milk, chocolate chips, cocoa powder, and sugar in a small saucepan over medium-low heat. Whisk gently until the chocolate is melted and the milk is frothy, about 5 minutes. Serve immediately, topped with whipped cream, if desired.

☀ MOGUL MINT MOCHA

This minty grown-up version of hot chocolate makes for a sweet after-dinner treat or a late-afternoon warmer-upper.

Prepare Rich Hot Chocolate, above, adding 4 teaspoons crème de menthe and 1 tablespoon coffee liqueur before topping with whipped cream.

MAKES 1 DRINK

1 cup milk

$1/4$ cup semisweet chocolate chips

1 teaspoon unsweetened cocoa powder

1 teaspoon sugar

Whipped cream (optional)

● hot apple cider

PRESIDENT JOHN ADAMS began each day with a hard cider beverage. He may not have skied afterward, however. We recommend adding the Calvados or applejack only after the lifts stop turning.

Heat the apple cider, cinnamon sticks, cloves, and orange slices in a medium saucepan over medium-high heat. Bring to a simmer and cook for 5 minutes. Turn off the heat and stir in the Calvados, if using. Serve immediately.

SERVES 5

1 (32-ounce) jug apple cider

3 (3-inch) cinnamon sticks

1 teaspoon cloves

1 orange, sliced

1 cup Calvados or applejack
  (optional)

■ hand-warmer hot buttered rum

WHEN YOUR FINGERS START to go numb from the cold, we recommend this drink instead of those hand warmers you drop into your mittens. While the traditional hand warmers are clever, this beverage warms a larger percentage of your body. You'll feel toasty in no time.

1. In a small bowl, thoroughly combine the butter and sugar. Refrigerate until almost firm, about 10 minutes.

2. Bring 4 cups water to a boil in a saucepan.

3. Place a cinnamon stick in each of 4 mugs. Add $\frac{1}{4}$ cup rum to each and fill to just below the rim with boiling water. Top evenly with the butter mixture. Stir with the cinnamon sticks and serve immediately.

SERVES 4

3 tablespoons unsalted butter,
  softened

3 tablespoons light brown sugar

4 (3-inch) cinnamon sticks

1 cup dark rum

NOTES AND TIPS FOR HIGH-ALTITUDE COOKING

Sunday River, Maine	780 feet
Stowe, Vermont	1,280
Whistler Blackcomb, British Columbia	2,140
Sun Valley, Idaho	5,750
Jackson Hole, Wyoming	6,200
Squaw Valley, California	6,310
Vail, Colorado	8,120
Alta, Utah	8,530
Taos, New Mexico	9,200

YOU PROBABLY LEARNED in high school chemistry class that water boils at 212°F. Like many of the things we learned in high school, the truth is a little more complicated. While 212°F is indeed the boiling point of water— at sea level—at high altitudes, water boils at a lower temperature.

Unfortunately, this has implications for the mountain cook beyond nerdy party tricks with the instant-read thermometer. Altitude robs moisture from foods. With less air pressure to constrain them, the characteristic air bubbles that define boiling burst at a more rapid rate. Thus, the liquid dissipates faster during the cooking process, leaving food dry. Even experienced cooks are sometimes flummoxed by adjusting their favorite recipes for high-altitude cooking. In a worst-case scenario, the result is tough muffins, undercooked pasta, and dried-out entrées.

But don't panic yet. With just a little thought, you can achieve a successful menu.

The first pertinent question: How high up are you? For simplicity's sake, all the recipes in this cookbook were tested between sea level and 2,500 feet. No adjustments need to be made below 3,000 feet. This covers most of the skiing on the East Coast and even some on the West Coast. The chart below shows a few popular ski destinations and the altitude at the base lodge.

Cooks who spend a lot of time at high altitudes find that trial and error are essential to fearless cooking and baking. If you'll be at altitude for just a few days, it makes more sense to plan your menu around this problem rather than learning a lot about creating delicate soufflés at 9,000 feet. Rather than stressing out about liquid adjustments, choose fast-cooking dishes that require no adjustment—like pan-seared pork chops or steaks. For dessert, choose ice cream with a homemade hot fudge or caramel sauce. Save the baking for a later date.

That said, countless mountain cooks use standard cookbooks without adjustment and do just fine. One friend, who lives at 6,000 feet, says she never adjusts ingredients, even in baking, but checks doneness religiously beginning halfway through the cooking time. Here is a review of different sorts of cooking and the altitude implications.

GENERAL COOKING

Many quickly prepared foods need little in the way of adjustment, even at the highest altitudes. Just as at sea level, you'll want to be sure to get the skillet nice and hot before adding the meat. You want to cook food as quickly as possible so it does not dry out.

If you're simmering a soup, be sure to lift the lid and stir frequently. Thick soups are especially susceptible to sticking to the bottom of the pot. As liquid condenses on the lid and drips back into the pot, you'll have a watery consistency at the top of the soup and a thick one at the bottom. A quick stir prevents this problem.

Slow cooking remains a useful method at altitude, but you may want to take a couple of precautions. Be sure to use the higher heat setting on your slow cooker. Expect food to take up to two hours longer to cook. If you're cooking above 5,000 feet, put a sheet of foil across the top of the pot or slow cooker, then place the lid over that. The foil will reflect heat into the pot and help maintain a higher temperature.

BOILING AT ALTITUDE

For every 400 or so feet above sea level, the boiling point of water drops approximately 1°F. At 7,000 feet, water boils at 199°F, and so on. When you set a pot of water on the stove and turn on the heat, the water temperature begins to rise. This increase in heat continues until you reach the local boiling temperature, at which point you'll see the characteristic bubbles rising to the surface that define boiling.

If you continue to apply heat to the bottom of the pot, something funny happens: The water in the pot boils, but it does not continue to get hotter. Instead, the bubbles grow larger and break faster, dissipating more of the boiling water into steam. Because the temperature determines cooking time (things cook faster at a higher temperature), the pasta or rice you boil on a high peak will cook slowly. While you wait, the water in the pot evaporates into the kitchen.

At very high altitudes, cooking pasta can be frustrating. You may find yourself adding water to the pot, which will cool the water further. The food seems to take forever to cook. Make sure you start with a very large pot of rapidly boiling water; don't skimp on the size of the pot. If you're not known for your patience, try buying fresh pasta—either frozen or refrigerated—instead of dried. Fresh pasta has a higher moisture content than dried and takes less time to cook.

Rice also takes longer. Try keeping a kettle of boiling water on the stove while your rice is cooking. Should you need to add water to replace what's evaporated, use water from the kettle to maintain a consistent cooking temperature. Couscous is less frustrating than rice, since it is parboiled. At altitude, it remains the quick and easy food it has always been at sea level.

When making soups, check the texture a bit more frequently than you might otherwise. If the soup reduces too quickly, add water 1/2 cup at a time, and stir frequently to avoid a crust forming.

BAKING

The most noticeable effect altitude has in the kitchen is on baking. The liquids in your batter tend to disappear before the food is cooked, which can be disastrous if you're at a very high altitude and make no changes to a recipe. Your baked goods dry out because the liquids boil away; this in turn concentrates the glutens, sugars, and leaveners in the rest of the ingredients. Your muffins are dry, overly sweet, and perhaps fallen if you made no adjustments.

To avoid these problems, proportions must be amended. While trial and error is the best way to find perfection, you can probably prevail by using the table below.

Be sure your baking powder and baking soda are fresh. This is a good rule for all baking, but if you're taking pains to reduce the amount you use, be sure the portion you retain is maximally active.

Finally—don't panic! Others have been here before. Just as your body will adjust to the altitude, so will your cooking. Take it slow and easy, and you'll get where you need to go.

	4,000 FEET	5,000 FEET	6,000 FEET	7,000 FEET	8,000 FEET	9,000 FEET
WATER BOILS AT	205°F	203°F	201°F	199°F	197°F	195°F
DECREASE BAKING POWDER PER TEASPOON BY (PERCENT)	1/8 teaspoon (13%)	scant 1/4 teaspoon (20%)	heaping 1/4 teaspoon (33%)	3/8 teaspoon (38%)	1/2 teaspoon (50%)	5/8 teaspoon (63%)
INCREASE LIQUID PER CUP BY (PERCENT)	1 tablespoon (6%)	2 tablespoons (13%)	3 tablespoons (19%)	4 tablespoons (25%)	5 tablespoons (31%)	6 tablespoons (38%)
DECREASE SUGAR PER CUP BY (PERCENT)	No change	1 teaspoon (3%)	2 teaspoons (5%)	1 tablespoon (7%)	1 1/2 tablespoons (10%)	2 tablespoons (13%)

STOCKING THE PANTRY, REFRIGERATOR, AND FREEZER

It's always a good idea to date whatever you are storing, particularly if you have a house for more than one season. Label the container before you put it away, and pay attention to expiration dates on packages. Replace spices after six months; discard freezer items after three months.

IDEALLY, your pantry would resemble your local grocery store, where everything you could ever want is at your fingertips. In reality, it's probably more like your medicine cabinet, full of expired products but missing a few necessities. With a thoughtfully stocked pantry, you'll find it easier to create each meal. You will need just a few fresh items to round out each recipe. We provide a guideline for stocking the essentials in your pantry so when the dinner bell rings, you'll have the ingredients you need to craft the perfect wintertime dish.

Some foods keep better than others, and we strive to stock those ingredients whenever possible. Modern technology has intervened, in some cases, to help. For example, peas freeze exceptionally well, and we use frozen peas to green up many a recipe. Frozen potatoes and carrots, though, are inferior to fresh at any time of year. Fortunately, these are widely available year-round in good quality. Some ingredients are stored more conservatively at our ski house due to infrequent attention. For example, we freeze butter to assure freshness, whereas we'd store it in the refrigerator at home, where we use it more quickly.

Beyond simply stashing your grocery items in the cupboard, freezer, or refrigerator, we recommend having airtight containers on hand for a longer shelf life and to act as a barrier against unwanted critters and freezer burn.

PANTRY STAPLES

Bread crumbs, panko • Store in the refrigerator after the package is opened.

Broth, low-sodium chicken and beef • We have 32-ounce cartons on hand for soups and 14-ounce cans for sauces. The cartons can also be frozen for longer storage.

Canned chipotle chiles in adobo sauce • Keeps indefinitely. Freeze the unused portion in a plastic container.

Capers • Refrigerate after opening. Keeps up to three months.

Cornstarch • Sits on the pantry shelf until we need it to thicken sauces. Keeps indefinitely.

Crackers, graham • Airtight bags in the pantry prevent sogginess, but we have been known to toast stale crackers in the oven during a s'mores emergency.

Dijon mustard • Refrigerate after opening. Keeps for a long time, but loses flavor after a couple of months.

Jam • Refrigerate after opening. Keeps several months.

Maple syrup • Refrigerate. Great flavoring for granola, sauces, and, of course, pancakes.

Mayonnaise • Refrigerate after opening.

Membrillo • Store in refrigerator.

Oils: extra-virgin olive oil, grapeseed oil, canola oil, and vegetable oil • Store away from the stove in a cool, dark place.

Olives, kalamata • The jarred and canned varieties keep indefinitely in the pantry.

Pastas: dried spaghetti, cut shapes • Buy a few extra boxes to prevent a pantry emergency.

Peanut butter • Commercial jarred peanut butters keep indefinitely.

Pickles, dill • The jarred variety keeps indefinitely in the pantry.

Popcorn • Keeps two years in an airtight container.

Rice, long-grained and Arborio • Store in an airtight container. Keeps indefinitely.

Salsa • Refrigerate. Keeps five days after jar is opened.

Soy sauce • Refrigerate after opening.

Tortillas, corn or flour • Refrigerate for up to two weeks, or freeze between layers of wax paper for longer storage.

Vinegars: white and red balsamic, red and white wine • The sweeter the vinegar, the quicker it can spoil. Generally these keep for months in a cool cupboard. A sniff test will tell you when it is time to buy a new bottle.

Wine, red and white • Keep on hand for sauces and unexpected guests.

DRIED HERBS AND SPICES

These keep up to a year in their airtight jars. Dried herbs and spices will, however, begin to weaken in flavor after three months.

Bay leaves

Cayenne

Chili powder

Cinnamon (ground and sticks)

Cloves

Coriander (ground)

Cumin

Curry powder

Ginger (fresh or ground)

Nutmeg (fresh or ground)

Oregano (dried or fresh)

Red pepper flakes

Rosemary (dried or fresh)

Salt and pepper: kosher and sea salts, black peppercorns

Thyme (dried or fresh)

BAKING NEEDS

Baking powder • Keeps one year in the pantry. Mix 1 teaspoon baking powder with $1/2$ cup hot water to test for freshness. If it bubbles vigorously, it is still good.

Baking soda • Keeps eighteen months in the pantry.

Chocolate: unsweetened, bittersweet, semisweet chocolate bars and chocolate chips • White residue on chocolate is not a problem, just a sign of exposure to uneven temperatures during storage. Store in airtight bags. Keeps indefinitely.

Cocoa, unsweetened • Store in airtight containers. You can substitute 3 tablespoons cocoa for 1 ounce unsweetened (baking) chocolate by adding 1 tablespoon butter or vegetable oil to most recipes. Keeps indefinitely.

Cornmeal • Store in airtight containers. Keeps indefinitely.

Espresso powder • Equally good as an ingredient in baking and drinking. Keeps indefinitely.

Flaked coconut • Store in airtight containers. Keeps six months.

Flour, all-purpose and whole wheat • Store in airtight containers to prevent insect infestation. All-purpose flour keeps indefinitely. Whole wheat should be kept in the freezer if you need to store it for longer than one month.

Honey • Store in airtight containers. Keeps indefinitely.

Oatmeal • Store in airtight containers. Keeps indefinitely.

Sugar, granulated and light brown • Keeps indefinitely. Because brown sugar dries out easily, store it, well wrapped, in the freezer to maintain moisture.

Vanilla extract • Keeps twelve months.

Wheat germ • Store in the refrigerator.

DAIRY

Cheeses (hard): Parmesan, Asiago, aged Cheddar, manchego, Gruyère • Many seem to keep forever, especially if vacuum packed. If you find yourself using shredded cheeses frequently, try freezing the shredded product in airtight storage bags. In many cases, you will not need to defrost the shredded cheese before adding it to the recipe.

Eggs • Refrigerate in the main compartment, not the door. Keep three weeks in the shell. Eggs are one item that is usable longer than the date on the package. To test for freshness, put an egg in a cup of water. If it floats, throw it out.

Heavy cream • Refrigerate. Alternatively, freeze. Defrost for recipes where the cream will be cooked. Keeps much longer than milk, so you'll have this on hand for your next dessert in a week or two.

Milk • Refrigerate. Try organic milk, which is super-pasteurized, for shelf life up to a month (check the expiration date).

Sour cream • Refrigerate. Keeps two weeks.

Yogurt • Refrigerate. Keeps seven to ten days.

MEAT AND FISH

Bacon • Freeze. We use this for a big breakfast but also as a flavoring for soups, pastas, and side dishes. For the easiest use in cooking, unwrap the bacon, rewrap in four-strip increments, and freeze in a freezer bag.

Chicken breast, boneless, skinless • For the height of convenience, freeze these individually in sealable plastic bags. You can defrost them in mere minutes in a warm water bath. Double-bagged meats will keep for three months.

Ground meats: beef, pork, turkey, and sausage • Freeze in small portions for easy defrosting. The more carefully wrapped, the longer the meat will stay appealing. Double-bagged meats will keep for three months. Vacuum-packed portions will keep even longer.

Ham steak • Refrigerate. Vacuum-packed products can keep for a month. Check the sell-by date on the packaging.

Steaks and chops • Freeze. Quick to defrost, especially when packed individually. Vacuum-packed portions will keep for months.

Tuna, canned and packed in olive oil • A pantry staple, and no more fattening than the less tasty version packed in water. Check the expiration date.

FRUITS AND VEGETABLES

Beans • We use canned black beans for Mexican dishes, white and pinto beans for soups and dips, red kidney beans for chili, and refried beans for an emergency side dish.

Berries: frozen blueberries and frozen mixed berries • Blueberries freeze exceptionally well.

Carrots • These last a month in the refrigerator.

Celery • Lasts weeks in the refrigerator.

Dried fruit: cranberries, raisins, apricots, currants • Easy to refresh with steam.

Dried legumes: white beans, split peas, and lentils • Great for soups. They keep forever.

Garlic • Keep in a cool dark area. Garlic is still usable in a pinch if it sprouts green at the top, but remove this bitter sprout. Discard the garlic if it feels soft when pinched or smells acrid.

Lemons • These keep in the refrigerator for a surprisingly long time before beginning to wither from dryness.

Onions • Keep two weeks or longer in a cool place, such as an unheated mudroom or basement.

Potatoes • Keep two weeks or longer before sprouting.

Shallots • Keep in a cool, dark area.

Tomatoes: canned whole, diced/crushed, and paste • We always have these on hand for soups and sauces.

Green vegetables • Peas and spinach freeze the best (and we use them in many recipes), followed by corn, green beans, and other legumes.

FROZEN NECESSITIES

Applesauce • If you have made a fresh batch, freeze to preserve for next time.

Baked bread • Freeze for two to three months; warm in a 400°F oven.

Butter • Freeze to avoid rancidity.

Coffee • Freeze for longer storage.

Ice cream • To avoid freezer burn, place a layer of plastic wrap on the surface of the ice cream before replacing the lid. Round containers with a separate lid seal better than flip-top boxes.

Nuts and seeds: almonds, walnuts, pecans, pignoli, sesame seeds, sunflower seeds, pumpkin seeds • Store in the refrigerator or freezer for freshness. The high fat content in nuts makes them prone to rancidity.

Pastas: ravioli or tortellini • Add just four minutes or so to the cooking time. Do not defrost before boiling, as they may stick together.

Pizza dough • Freeze for one month; allow plenty of time to defrost.

Puff pastry • Keep in freezer until ready to use.

EQUIPMENT

SO YOU'RE ALL READY for a week of great powder skiing and relaxing by the fireplace. You've booked the condo, dug out your goggles, packed your recipes, and shopped for the ingredients. After your first day on the mountain, you deserve to relax with a sweet treat. Just when you've added the last ingredient to your bowl of brownie batter, you realize you don't have any baking pans! Rather than leave you licking the bowl (not that there's anything wrong with that), we've put together a basic list of kitchen tools to refer to when planning your getaways.

Whether renting a weekend condo or a seasonal house, don't assume anything about the kitchen. You can always phone ahead to find out how it is stocked. Most come equipped with the bare essentials: a range, a microwave, plates, silverware, a few pots and pans, a toaster, a coffeemaker, a refrigerator, and a few cooking utensils. You might think it's enough until you actually start cooking and realize there are no mixing bowls, spatulas, or nonstick skillets. We don't suggest packing your entire kitchen; we simply aim to remind you of what you might want to have on hand.

Another way to think about this is to play a sort of ski house version of "if I were stranded on a desert island." We'll do it this way: If we were snowed in at a ski-on, ski-off chalet in Aspen, these are the items we would want to have.

TOOLS AND UTENSILS

Can opener • A commonly forgotten but necessary item.

Colander • Although we prefer stainless steel, plastic works just fine. We use these for draining pasta or washing and drip-drying vegetables. If you find yourself without one, you can always carefully tip a full pot into the sink, using the lid of the pot to hold back the contents while letting the water escape. Go slowly unless you want your meal to swirl down the drain.

Corkscrew • Self-explanatory and essential!

Cutting board • This is often overlooked in the remember-to-ask category. Any rental property that omits this will probably not mind if you use a plate instead, but this will dull your knife and slow down your work. Wood is best, but plastic is fine.

Grater • We use this for cheese but also for grating vegetables when necessary. We use it so often we always tuck one into our suitcase.

Immersion blender • We can't say enough about this gizmo. It is small—small enough to toss into our overnight bag for a weekend away. It's inexpensive—$30 buys a decent one. There are a million ways to use this appliance. The most obvious use is to puree soups and sauces, but most come with attachments that allow the speedy mincing of vegetables and whipping of eggs or other liquids. If we were snowed in at our fantasy chalet, this would be the first item in our stash.

Instant-read thermometer • We like to have a meat thermometer nearby, particularly if we're using an unfamiliar oven. Cooking times are a great guideline for doneness, but a thermometer allows you to be exact.

Knives • We also make room in our bag for the two most valuable knives: an 8-inch chef's knife and a 3½-inch paring knife. A serrated bread knife is also helpful but you can live without it for a weekend.

Measuring cups and spoons • It's a little tough to get much done without these essential tools. Bring a set of four cups (¼, ⅓, ½, 1 cup) for dry measuring and a 1-cup and/or 2-cup glass or plastic measuring cup with a spout for wet ingredients. In case of emergency, remember that a 1-ounce shot glass can be used to measure out ⅛ cup, which is also 2 tablespoons or 6 teaspoons. Measuring spoons will fit into your pocket—better safe than sorry.

Mixing bowls • A set of three sizes is the most useful for general food and baking preparation. In a pinch, try cutting down an empty gallon milk jug.

Pepper grinder • Seeing that we call for fresh pepper in a majority of recipes, this is an extremely useful tool.

Spatulas • Whether for scraping out a batter bowl or for cooking in nonstick pans, a rubber spatula can be a cook's best friend. You will also need a flat metal or plastic spatula for those early-morning pancakes.

Vegetable peeler • If you're experienced with knives, you can use a paring knife to do the work of a peeler, but most folks end up cutting away more than just the peel.

Whisk • We love to have at least one whisk on hand to remove lumps in batters and sauces and to whip up vinaigrettes. When we don't have one, we use a fork.

Wooden spoons • If you're stocking a kitchen for the season, grab a few of these; you'll be happy you did. We particularly like to use them when making soups, stews, and sauces. And you can't beat the $1 price tag.

Zester • This gadget is the best way to zest a piece of citrus. If you buy a decent one, it's also great for grating cheese over pasta.

OVEN AND STOVETOP

Baking/cake pans • We call for 9-inch round cake pans and an 8-inch square pan.

Baking dishes and casseroles • Although some people use these terms interchangeably, a casserole dish is generally measured in quarts, can be round or oval, and comes with a lid. A baking dish is a shallow, rectangular or oval dish measured in inches. Both are generally made of glass or ceramic, and we find it most useful to have a 9 x 13-inch dish and a 3-quart lidded dish. We make baked casseroles (and brownies) in these, and we also use them for serving.

Baking sheets • Also referred to as sheet pans or cookie sheets, these rectangular, rimmed pans can be used to roast vegetables or to bake free-form pies and cookies.

Cooling racks • These are a baker's friend for cooling cakes and cookies but can also be used as a kind of trivet to allow dishes to cool down quickly and evenly.

Dutch oven • Although a large saucepan can handle many tasks, we make soup and boil pasta in this when we need the space. If you plan a lot of meals around slow-braising meat, either in the oven or on the stovetop, a Dutch oven is the perfect wintertime companion.

Muffin tins • Obviously, you need a muffin tin only if you plan on making muffins, but it also comes in handy when you have a lot of chopping to do. Use it as a means to keep your prepped vegetables organized and separated.

Saucepans • Having a few sizes (2-quart, 4-quart, or 6- to 8-quart) allows you to melt a stick of butter or make a big pot of soup. If we had to pick just one, it would be a 6-quart pan.

Skillets/sauté pans • We like having one nonstick skillet for making food such as omelets and one regular skillet for creating a perfectly brown sear on meat. A 10- to 12-inch pan is ideal. If you're stocking a house for the season, cast iron is a functional and inexpensive way to do it.

Slow cooker • Where would we be without this? Not only is it an energy saver, but it holds a lot of food, which is great when we've invited a crowd. It is, however, heavy. If you find yourself braising foods without it, you can use your oven at a very low temperature. But then you'll need some big oven-proof pots.

MISCELLANEOUS

Blender • Not just for strawberry daiquiris. Blenders are perfect for pureeing soups, sauces, and salad dressings.

Cocktail shaker • Perfect for après-ski drinks. We never leave home without one.

Coffeemaker • You'll need it, whether for coffee drinks or just to wake up in the morning. Make sure to ask your rental property if you'll have one.

Plastic food storage bags • These are useful not just for storing miscellaneous leftovers but also for freezing food for future visits.

Storage containers • You'll want something to stash your leftovers in overnight. If you have a ski house for a season, you'll also want to seal your dry goods in airtight containers.

Thermos • A welcome companion if you bring your lunch to the mountain. We like it for soups and stews as well as for an extra jolt of coffee in the morning.

INDEX

Note: **Boldfaced** page references indicate photographs.